COMPACT CYMRU

On the trail of the Welsh Drovers

Twm Elias

Gwasg Carreg Gwalch

First published in 2018
© text: Twm Elias
© publication: Gwasg Carreg Gwalch 2018

ISBN: 978-1-84524-282-4

Cover design: Eleri Owen

Published by Gwasg Carreg Gwalch,
12 Iard yr Orsaf, Llanrwst, Wales LL26 0EH
tel: 01492 642031
email: books@carreg-gwalch.cymru
website: www.carreg-gwalch.cymru

Acknowledgements

Images by Jean Napier: 8(2), 9, 17(3), 19, 32, 59,
68(1), 125(1)
Image by Keith O'Brien: 29
National Library of Wales: 25(1&2), 29(2&3), 39
Emlyn Richards: 35(2)
R. Avent: 76
Northampton Library: 78

Cover image: Pont Scethin, Rhinogydd
Image page 1: Over the Migneint moors to
Ysbyty Ifan
Below: Llandecwyn church overlooking the
Dwyryd estuary (Traeth Bach) on the old
Harlech to Maentwrog road

Contents

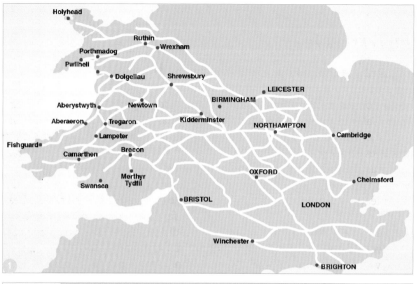

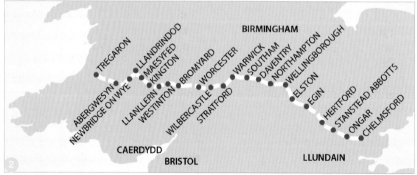

1. The general pattern of drove routes from Wales to England in the pre-railway era;
2. Route taken by the Jonathan family of Dihewyd from Tregaron to Chelmsford,
October 1839. The journey took 3 weeks.

Haip! Trrrrw-how!
On the Trail of the Welsh Drovers

Before the coming of the railways to north and west Wales in the middle of the 19th century the only method of moving cattle, sheep and even geese to distant English markets was to walk them. Those who undertook that task were the drovers, accompanied by a few hardy helpers and dogs.

The successful drover had to be a strong, well organised and amiable character, well able to think on his feet and respond to unforeseen situations as they arose. He needed considerable skills in handling people and animals at every stage of the journey and needed a good business head; to buy from a set of hard-bargaining farmers at one end and to sell at the other end to graziers who could be just as tough in price negotiations.

It is difficult for us today to perceive the logistics, difficulties and dangers of walking a drove of up to 200 cattle from Pembrokeshire to Kent or over a thousand sheep from Caernarfonshire to Essex. Such journeys would have presented considerable challenges – travelling 12-14 miles a day for up to three weeks; staying overnight in various inns and arriving on time ahead of certain targeted fairs or markets.

But that would not have been the end of the story. Having delivered the beasts to the far end without mishap and in good condition, the drove now needed to be sold for the best price in one of the numerous fairs in the English Midlands or the Home Counties, including the great 'Welsh Fair' in Barnet, or as far as Maidstone in Kent, and the money brought back safely.

The risks were certainly greater on the return journey because the drover would now be carrying the sales money which could amount to several hundred pounds in gold. This tended to generate an interest from certain undesirable quarters and there are some very dramatic stories of encounters with thieves and highway robbers. The drovers, however, were professionals who were fully aware of the

risks and knew how to avoid or minimise danger and take appropriate action when necessary. They were frequently armed, were accompanied by big dangerous dogs and whenever possible arranged to travel home in a gang of fellow drovers for protection.

The beasts chosen for the journey would have been store animals; cattle and sheep in good condition but not fattened. The drover's skill lay in selecting the right animals, which would have been those tough enough for the journey and which suited the graziers who bought them at the other end. Graziers in the English Midlands and Home Counties would pay good prices for the right animals and the drover's art was to supply beasts which would be lean, fit and with shiny coats after their exertion. Basically, what the graziers needed were the 'frames' since their good pastures would soon put on the meat. The animals would then be sold fat over the next few months or even up to a year to butchers in nearby cities and towns.

1. H Tennant 1806, 'Welsh Drovers crossing a river'; 2. Thomas Rowland 1797, 'Llangollen Hill on the road to Ruthin'

Drovers obtained their animals either in local fairs, sometimes spread over two or three counties or, preferably, directly from the farms which, again, could involve traveling over a wide area. Buying in fairs usually meant payment in cash while procuring beasts from the farms meant that they could usually be taken on credit, which had the benefit of avoiding large cash outlays. They could also have first choice of the animals most likely to sell well and would endeavour to establish a regular business relationship with the suppliers of such animals as well as good customers at the other end.

A good name coupled with a reputation for honesty and fair dealing was vital to win the trust of farmers and customers alike. A poem by the Vicar Pritchard in 1681 instructs drovers on the virtues of keeping to the straight and narrow:

> Os'dwyt borthmon delia'n onest
> Tâl yn gywir am a gefaist
> Cadw d'air, na thor d'addewid
> Gwell nag aur mewn cod yw credid.[1]

If you're a drover deal honestly
Pay correctly for what you received

Twm o'r Nant, the 18th century Interlude writer wrote a singeing 'englyn' (strict meter 4-liner) on the death of one drover who had displeased him:

Yma mae hen borthmon yn huno – difaodd
*   Ei fywyd ar dwyllo:*
*   Aeth ef o'i fyd i'w grŷd gro;*
*   Twll ei dîn, twylled yno.*

Here an old drover lies – he wasted
        His life by cheating:
    He left this world for a gravelly bed;
    Arseholes to him, let him cheat there.

Needless to say, this englyn was not inscribed on the drover's headstone.[3]

Keep your word, don't break a promise
Better than gold in a purse is credit.

The 'credit' that the good Vicar referred to in the last line would have been that redeemable in Heaven.

There were, however, a few rogues especially in the early days of droving. A Medieval Welsh proverb states:

'*Tri pheth nid hawdd eu coeliaw: llw porthmon, addewid gordderchwr, a gair heliwr am ei gi.*'[2]

Three things not easily believed: a drover's oath, an adulterer's promise and a huntsman's word about his dog.

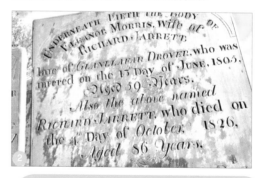

1. H Bartlett, The old Harlech road; 2. A drover's gravestone, Trawsfynydd; 3. Old map of the Welshpool to Caernarfon road

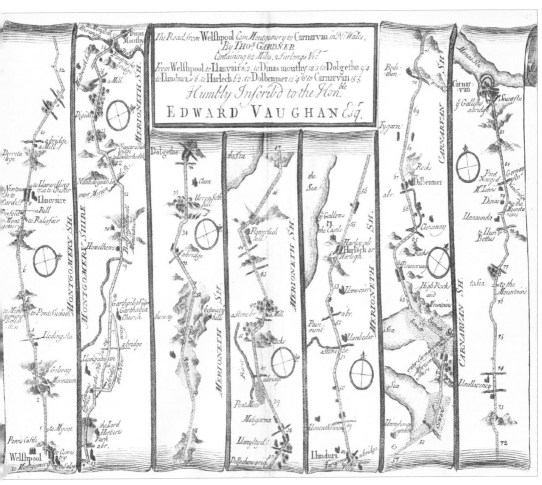

The Road from **Welshpool** Com Montgomery to **Carnarvan** in N: Wales.
By **Thos GARDNER**
Containing 82 Miles, 2 Furlongs Viz
From Welshpool to Llanvair 8,2. to Dinas mouthy 18,3. to Dolgethe 9,4
to Llandwa in 6. to Harlech 6,2. to Dolbenmer 12,4 to Carnarvan 15,6

Humbly Inscrib'd to the Hon.ble

EDWARD VAUGHAN *Esq*

The historical background

Because of the scarcity of written records it is difficult to say when commercial droving from Wales to England began as opposed to the driving of cattle or sheep from one area to another and between winter and summer pastures.

It is probable that cattle driving occurred during the Roman period, but over what distances we do not know. The Romans came here not for the weather but to get rich through exploiting resources and extracting taxes, or Tribute, which native people were obliged to pay. In a predominantly non-monetary economy the Tribute would have been payable in the form of metals, cattle, grain and slaves. Cattle and grain would be taken to feed local garrisons and probably, at times, moved along the road network to larger settlements.

Offa's Dyke, the late 8th century earthworks which formed a border between Wales and Mercia had a number of gaps along it where trade took place. It is interesting to speculate about the real reason for building the dyke. It certainly would not have been an effective barrier against a determined war party but would have prevented the movement of cattle. The Welsh were reputed to bring cattle to trade with the Mercians, only to send a raiding party to recover them at a later date. The dyke would have been an effective means of preventing that.

By the 13th century more reliable records exist, though not very numerous, indicating a regular trade with cattle being driven by Welsh drovers some distance into England. A yearly fair and weekly cattle-market were established at Newent, Gloucestershire in 1253 which would have facilitated this movement.[4]

Following Edward 1st's attempted subjugation of Wales, we see in the new Tax Extents in 1292/1293 for the townships of Nefyn and Llanbedr Pont Steffan (Lampeter) references to the occupation of 'porthmon' (drover).[5] Over a century later, in 1418, we find the first reference, again in a Tax Extent, to a named drover: Tegwared Porthmon in the Commote of Menai on Anglesey.[6]

In 1312, some 900 Welsh cattle were sent to the kitchens of Edward 2nd in

Windsor, following which a number of English nobles took advantage of the Royal Warrant to import Welsh cattle to supply their own households.[7]

During the 100 Year War (1337-1443) between England and France the Constables of the Welsh castles bought cattle to be driven to Southampton. There the animals were killed and the meat salted, put into barrels and shipped to feed the armies in France.[8]

Through the 14th-15th centuries the demand grew for Welsh cattle. They regularly appeared in fairs in Chester in the 1300s and occasionally as far as Barnett near London. In 1347, for example, 68 cattle were taken from Rhuthun and Abergele to Macclesfield. By the end of the 14th century the trade had become a flourishing business which was temporarily suspended by the English authorities during Owain Glyndwr's War of Independence in the early 1400s. This would have been a form of economic sanction against the Welsh. Cattle, however, continued to be moved from north-west Wales into western Cheshire during this time, albeit illicitly.[9]

Sir Edwin Landseer, ancient white cattle

Following that episode the cattle trade resumed and there are records, for example, of Welsh cattle in Birmingham fair in 1445 and of 33 cattle being walked from Wrexham to Suffolk in 1463. In that same period we have an interesting account in a 'cywydd' (long strict meter poem) by Guto'r Glyn, who took a drove of Tithe lambs on behalf of the Rector of

Corwen to England to sell. His journey took him as far as Chesterfield.[10]

A great boost to the Welsh cattle trade occurred following the success of Henry Tudor and his predominantly Welsh army at Bosworth in 1485. One of his first actions, as with any new regime taking power, was to appoint some of his trusted followers to important governmental positions. Many of the Welsh nobility who had supported the Tudor cause benefited and some moved to London and elsewhere to take up such positions, a tradition which continued throughout the Tudor Dynasty.

The Welsh nobles newly established in London soon began to take advantage of their situation and some arranged for cattle from their home estates to be brought to London to be sold. A thriving market for beef was to be found there and it became a convenient way of transferring rent moneys to the Welsh nobles 'on the hoof'.

Following the Acts of Union, 1536 and 1542, the legal and economic restrictions on Wales, which had been in place for over two and a half centuries were finally abolished. This ushered in a golden age for the Welsh drovers who could now, under licence, take cattle and get good prices for them in large market towns like Bristol, Birmingham, Manchester, Northampton and London. The market records for Shrewsbury, between 1563 and 1600, record the selling of cattle from Caernarfonshire and most of the other counties of north and mid Wales. Estate papers reveal a similar story, for example cattle, sheep and geese being driven from Wales to the Earl of Gloucester's estate at Kenilworth in 1575 and cattle to Lord Dudley in Kent in 1584.[11]

John Dee, one of Elisabeth 1st's main advisers describes sending his servant on more than one occasion to bring cattle from Wales and when he was appointed Warden of Manchester in 1596 how his relatives in Cardiganshire sent cattle to him in September of that year.

Drovers, from the Tudor period onwards, in order to ply their trade to England and avoid arrest under the vagrancy laws had to be licenced. To qualify, they had to be married householders of above 30 years of age and

1. John Dee, advisor to Queen Elisabeth 1st;
2. Castell Gwydir, Llanrwst;
3. Cattle arriving in London, 1598

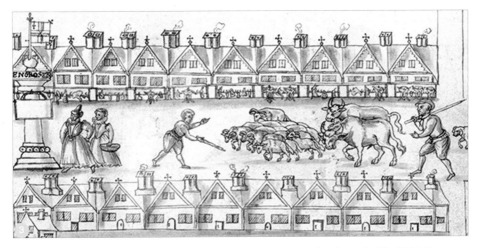

not hired servants. If they could fulfil these conditions and were "*known to be honest men of good sufficiency according to the statutes*" they could apply to their local Quarter Sessions for a licence which, if granted, would cost 12 pence plus a further 8 pence for registration. Licencing ensured a legal right to move across country and was also an attempt to prevent wrongdoing by a few "*...suspicious and base persons... who under cover of driving their droves... not only receive cattle stolen by thieves, but themselves do steal by way of other men's cattle and sheep.*"[12]

The papers of the Wynn family of Gwydir in the Conwy valley contain many references to cattle prices, payment to drovers and fairs to which their cattle were sent. In 1607 Sir John Wynn was asked by Elisabeth Spencer to send cattle to her via drovers to England while in 1624 a buyer from Kent, who usually bought Pembrokeshire cattle, wished also to buy from him.[13]

The Civil War in England impacted considerably on the cattle trade and created great difficulties for many. In his petition to Prince Rupert the Archbishop of York, John Williams of Conwy, asks for the unhindered movement of drovers and describes the cattle as: "*The Spanish Fleet of Wales, bringing what little gold and silver we have*". In 1644 when the Parliamentary forces impounded 900 cattle from Welsh drovers, compensation was duly paid and in 1645 special licenses were granted for movement across the military lines. This shows that, despite the war, both sides were as dependent as each other on the cattle trade.[14]

Sheep were also driven at this time, though not to the extent of cattle. When Richard Horsenaile in Essex died in 1690 he left 43 "*Welch sheep and lambs*", while Daniel Defoe in the 1720s describes Welsh sheep "*...driven hundreds of miles to the Home Counties to become London's mutton.*"

By the 18th century we are on the verge of substantial economic changes driven by burgeoning overseas trade and the dawn of the Industrial Revolution. Wealth and population was now increasing rapidly triggering an increasing demand for food. This led to a substantial increase in the numbers of Welsh cattle driven eastwards each summer and autumn, especially to Essex and Kent.

As population increased with the Industrial Revolution the need to feed the growing numbers necessitated an

Agricultural Revolution to walk hand in hand with it. Thus, from the 1740s onwards we see several pioneering developments to increase agricultural production and keep up with the growing demand for food. Some names stand out, for example Lord Townsend or 'Turnip' Townsend, who introduced new crops and systems from the Continent and Thomas Bakewell and others who were pioneers of improving farm animals by breeding. Townsend's 'Norfolk 4-course Rotation', which included new root crops was of special relevance to Wales since arable farms in central and south-eastern England could now keep far more animals over the winter than before, leading to a much greater demand for Welsh store cattle for fattening.

In 1780 it is estimated that the population of Britain was about 6 million, which by 1801 had increased to 9 million. London itself had grown from 60,000 in 1500 to 675,000 in 1750 and had reached a million by 1801. It was the biggest city in Europe at this time and with more than its fair share of merchants, professional people and the well to do, who could afford to eat more meat, including beef. In fact very little meat and hardly any beef was consumed by working people, as alluded to in the opening lines of a Welsh nursery rhyme:

Bachgen bach o Felin y Wig
Welodd o 'rioed damaid o gig...

A little boy from Melin y Wig
Had never seen a piece of meat...

In a letter to the Countess of Fingal in 1768, a young aristocrat, J Jackson, on a visit to Dolgellau, testified that beef was very scarce in the town as all the cattle were being bought by drovers to be driven to England, but it would be possible to obtain beef by bringing it in by coach from Shrewsbury.[15]

1. J C Reed 1863, 'Drovers near Beddgelert';
2. Rowlandson, 1840s, 'Drovers on the road;
3. Bwlch Drws Ardudwy through the Rhinogydd

More than droving

At a time when it could be difficult and dangerous for individuals to travel on their own, and when stagecoaches were often inconvenient and costly, drovers sometimes carried money and letters on behalf of the gentry and others or orders for goods on behalf of merchants. They preferred not to carry large sums because of the danger of robbery and would, instead, carry a bill of exchange which could be cashed by the recipient at the other end. A favoured method was to use the cash obtained to buy cattle at this end and to pay the recipient at the other end from the sales money, thus making a little profit from the deal.

The drover John Lloyd in the 1620s would transfer money from Sir John Wynn of Gwydir to his son in London. Forty years later the drover's son, David Lloyd, performed the same function, transferring £65 from Sir Richard Wynn to Robin Hughes through a bill of exchange to be paid through Henry Maurice at the King's Head tavern in Fleet Street, London.[16]

Rents were transferred to landlords in London and even taxes. A letter to Richard Bulkeley in 1637 from his cousin in Niwbwrch (Newborough), Anglesey states: "...*we pray you endeavour that our money* (i.e. the Ship Money) *be paid by November 1st yearly as we cannot return our money* (to London) *otherwise than by drovers.*"[17] The stage coach service would have ceased over the winter by this time and would not resume until the spring, so the drovers were the only hope of delivering the money to London. Failure to deliver on time incurred heavy penalties. The delivery of Ship Taxes from north Wales to London via drovers persisted until as late as 1743.

Rowland Edmunds from Felenrhyd near Maentwrog at the end of the 18th century took an order from a milliner in Harlech to a Mr Gould in London for cloth. The materials were duly shipped from the Port of London to a warehouse at Ynys, Talsarnau to be collected by the milliner. The money was paid exactly one year later when Rowland Edmunds came again to London with another drove of cattle.[18]

Religious materials were also

An old drove track on the Rhinogydd – nowadays a path for walkers

A London milestone on the drover's track along the Kerry Ridgeway

the Dolaucothi mines, to be sold to jewellers in London.

Travellers would sometimes accompany the droves, including students making their way from rural Wales to colleges in Oxford and Cambridge. John Jones of Cerrigydrudion (Jac Glan Gors) the radical poet and supporter of the French Revolution reached London in 1789 in this way and the artist Robert Hughes of Uwchlaw'rffynnon, Llŷn in 1843.

In Cardiganshire mostly a tradition developed in the 18th century for young girls to accompany the drovers to seek seasonal work in the extensive market gardens to the north of London or to pick fruit in the orchards of Kent. At the end of the 18th century it appears that a substantial proportion of the girls selling fruit, vegetables and flowers on the streets of London were from Wales. An old rhyme describes the scene:

> O na bawn i fel colomen
> Ar Sant Pawl yng nghanol Llunden
> I gael gweled merched Cymru
> Ar eu gliniau'n chwynu'r gerddi.

> O to be as a pigeon
> On Saint Paul in the middle of London

transferred. Among the papers of the Reverend Thomas Charles of Bala we find a letter dated 1794 from the Reverend Thomas Jones of Creaton, Northamptonshire requesting religious pamphlets to be sent via drovers. Similarly, Ellis Owen of Cefn-y-Meusydd, Penmorfa in 1834 sent money to the Bible Society in London via the drover Owen Williams.[19]

Small items such as knitted socks and lacework would be taken and sold, while some Cardiganshire drovers took gold, sometimes illegally taken by miners from

So I can see the girls of Wales
Kneeling to weed the gardens.

Drovers, being astute businessmen would sometimes use their large cash turnover to invest money in commercial ventures. The will of Rowland Edmunds of Maentwrog, who died in 1816, shows that he had part shares in a ship and several local businesses. Perhaps the most famed entrepreneur was Dafydd Jones of Llanymddyfri (1759-1839) who established the Black Ox Bank in 1799 and later became a High Sherriff of Carmarthenshire.

Drovers were often in a position to loan cash. When Silvanus Evans, a drover from Llan Ffestiniog died in 1911, he had a drawer full of gold and silver pocket-watches given to him as surety for loans, each with a slip of paper with the name of the debtor and sum owed inside.[20]

They would buy farms at home for use in their droving enterprises while other drovers bought farms in Northamptonshire when land was cheap during the agricultural depressions before the First World War and subsequently in the 1920s-30s. Many Cardiganshire drovers in the late 19th century became involved in setting up milk retail businesses from town dairies in London and elsewhere.[21]

Silvanus Evans, drover of Llan Ffestiniog (John Thomas, late 19th century)

Bringing news and ideas

At a time when travelling overland would have been confined mostly to aristocrats and vagrants, the drovers, plying their trade over long distances were founts of wondrous tales and valuable information. Their reports of what they had seen and heard would have amazed and entertained a rural population back home, many of whom, due to the confines of their farming routines, would seldom travel further than the nearest market town.

Drovers were the first to bring back news of the Napoleonic and other foreign wars; the progress through Parliament of the land-grabbing Enclosure Acts affecting common lands; technological and other developments; scandals; murders and highway robberies. They brought back small fashionable gifts for their wives and introduced ballad tunes while their less reputable helpers carried back swearwords.

They frequently brought useful information, such as tips for agricultural improvement, medical recipes and fruit seeds. It is said that the source of some old apple trees on upland farms in Cardiganshire were drovers returning from Kent or has passed through the Vale of Evesham. One drover in the 1840s saw am interesting clock in a shop window in London, bought the mechanism (not the body), wrapped it in a cloth and brought it home to a clockmaker friend in Tremadog, who copied elements of the workings into his own design. Some of these grandfather clocks survive today and are still keeping time.[22]

Many drovers were cultured and religious. They bought books and their names frequently crop up in the lists of subscribers to publications on poetry and religion. Edward Morus of Perthi Llwydion, Cerrigydrudion (1633?-1689) was one of the foremost poets of his era and died in Essex during a droving trip. Dafydd Jones of Cayo (1711-1777), returning home from England was so

1. Inside cover of a religious book owned by J Williams, Drws y Nant, bought 'in the Cloystars Near Smithfield'; 2. Memorial to the hymnwriter Dafydd Jones from Gaeo

captivated by the wonderful hymn-singing emanating from a Chapel he passed at Troed-rhiw-dalar in the old county of Breconshire, that he became a convert. He became one of our foremost hymn writers.

Others fell foul of the religious establishment because of their tendency to partake of alcoholic beverages when doing business with certain customers. Many Chapels in the 19th century and even up to the mid-20th century observed a strict tee-total rule. That is why a drover from Llanfrothen in the 1930s was stopped from being a Sunday-school teacher for occasionally lubricating his deals with a tot of whiskey. He was, however, reinstated, after several families stopped sending their children to Sunday school. Another drover in the late 19th century, after a number of warnings, was publically excommunicated in Llan Ffestiniog, having been seen entering a tavern. He left the congregation in disgrace, walked around the Chapel three times before re-entering to say he had repented. He was welcomed back with open arms as the prodigal son. He had to be much more careful from then on.

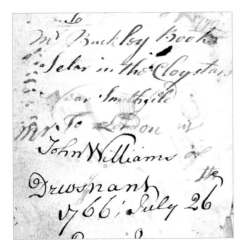

The art of the drover

The license issued in 1572 to Hughe ap Gruffudd from Llŷn to take cattle to England allowed him to practice '*ye mysterie and science of commen drovers*'.[23] An interesting statement; more of a skill than a mystery maybe, and the science would have been logistical. But it would certainly have needed some special qualities; to be able to handle men and beasts on their long journey, to sell well and bring the sales money home safely.

A good memory was an invaluable asset given the scale and complexity of their numerous transactions. Some drovers would regularly take animals to sell on behalf of the local estate and submit a detailed list of expenses – tollgates, overnight stops, beer and victuals en route – to be claimed back later from the agent of the estate. Such accounts are an invaluable source of information about routes and logistics. Apart from these instances, but with some notable exceptions, very few drover kept detailed accounts of their journeys and transactions. All such details were kept in their heads. They must have had incredible memories. Rowland Edmunds of Maentwrog was probably the most important drover in Merionethshire in the late 18th century, yet never put anything on paper as he was illiterate.[24]

1. *Portrait of a drover: William Price of Nercwys c1860; 2. Drovers licence issued to Hughe ap Gruffudd, 1572; 3. & 4. Parts of the Jonathan family accounts, 1840*

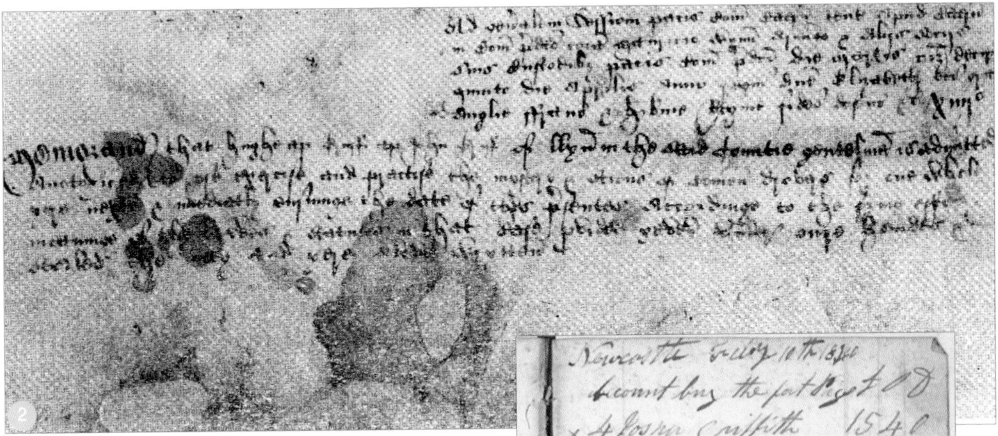

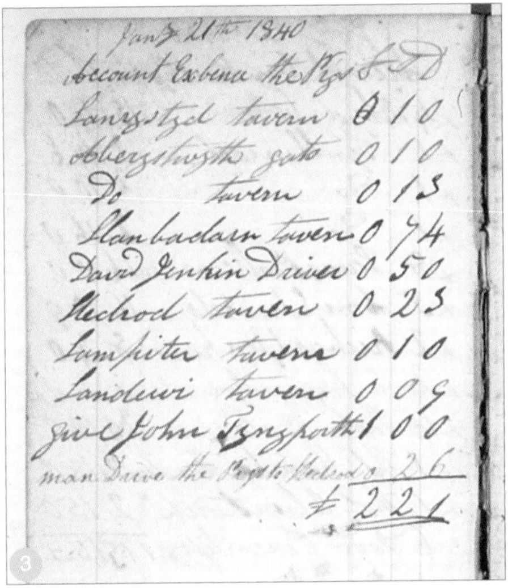

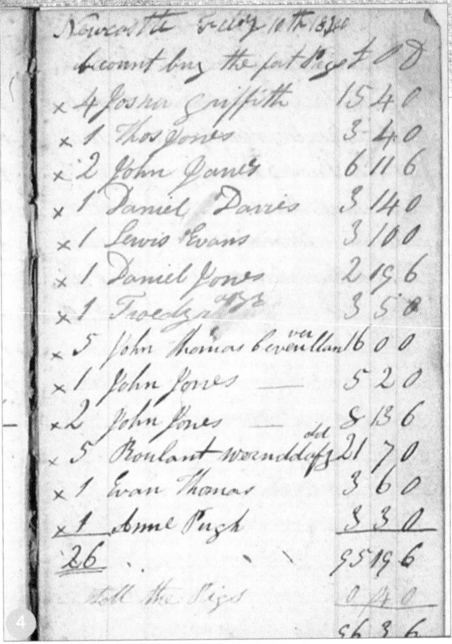

Procuring the beasts

Originally the drover or dealer would procure his animals from two main sources: directly from the farms or from fairs and markets. After the 1914-1918 War a third option, auction marts, strategically located at sites along the railways came to replace the old fairs.

On the farm – this was the preferred source of animals for the drover because he could usually take the animals on credit, which meant he didn't have to pay the farmer until he returned with the sales money. From the drover's point of view there were several advantages to this system:

- avoiding large cash outlays when buying.
- having the first choice of the animals best suited for the journey and most likely to sell well.

The drover could either take the beasts home to his own farm or ask the farmer to

1. Buying calves on the farm;
2. Sheep at Welshpool mart

hold on to them for a short while and bring them to a gathering point the day before the drove set off. This would often be a field hired for the purpose at a convenient location for the start of the drove.

An advantage for the farmer was that he could avoid the time and trouble of selling in a fair with its attendant uncertainties regarding prices. He, obviously, had to have confidence in the drover's integrity and ability to fulfil his (unwritten) contract and pay up as promised.

Animals would be taken not just from the larger farms but also from smaller farms or smallholdings from which an individual cow might be sold each year to pay the rent. There are many tales of how people would try to give the impression that the animal was worthy of a good price. One example is of an old lady near Dolgellau who had fattened an old beast and insisted that it had good quality yearling meat. The basis of her contention was that the animal was thin a few months ago but was now fat, so all the meat was new!

The drovers tended to have a regular set of suppliers at this end just as they often had a regular clientele in the Midlands. Graziers at that end, having received animals which had done particularly well in previous years would look to the drover who had supplied them for more of the same.

The accounts of John Jones, Plas yn Glascwm, Penmachno who was a sheep drover in the 1850s, shows he had regular circuits around farms in particular districts. Some were in his own and neighbouring valleys, e.g. Penmachno, Ysbyty Ifan and Ffestiniog. He also bought sheep from a number of farms on the northern side of the Mawddach Valley, some distance away to the south. He supplied a regular set of clients: mostly butchers in the new coastal tourist resorts of Llandudno and Colwyn Bay.[25]

There were instances of a drover's trust being abused. One concerns John Owen, a young Anglesey man who, in 1765 had bought cattle on credit, to the value of £200, then drove them to Barnet and Smithfield to be sold. He claimed, however, that on his way home he had been robbed near Dunstable. The evidence is a judicial letter, currently held by the Gwynedd Archive Service, to the Rector of Llanddaniel parish enquiring about the boy's age. Suspicions were aroused and a substantial portion of the 'lost' money was found in boy's possession. In the trial which followed, the boy's age was crucial. If he was over 21 and therefore an adult, he would undoubtedly have been hung. But if he was below 21 he would be considered by the court to be a minor and the onus would have been on the farmers for trusting someone so young and unlicensed. There is no record of a hanging, so the Rector presumably found in the boy's favour.

Fairs – one need only look in the various Almanacs published from the late 18th century to the early 20th century to see how numerous were the village and town fairs in every one of the old counties. Some villages might have held only one, two or three fairs annually, while some larger centres or towns might have held half a dozen or more, plus weekly markets, which would be venues for seasonal animal sales. The success of fairs could vary considerably from year to year, dependent on the number of buyers who attended and the quality of the stock on offer after drovers had possibly already taken the best directly from the farms.

After haggling, agreeing a price and striking hands to seal the contract, cash would exchange hands for the animals bought, with a small sum being given back as 'luck money'. After purchase the beasts would be turned into a sale field until they were ready to be taken away, having being marked in some way by the drover, commonly by cutting a simple identifying mark in the hair on the flank with a small scissors to show ownership.

Drovers wishing to take advantage of these fairs would travel to the far reaches of two or three counties to buy the stock they required and would arrange to visit a number of fairs in sequence. Thus, having bought cattle in the fair at Sarn Meillteyrn on the Llŷn peninsula on the first day, they would be walked to Pwllheli where more animals would be purchased at a fair held there the following day. Yet more could be accumulated on the way home.

The accounts of the Jonathan family of Dihewyd, Cardiganshire for the 1830s-40s show how they regularly started buying

1. List of fairs in Meirionnydd, from Almanac Caergybi 1876; 2. Silvanus Evans (centre) striking a deal; 3. Llanerchymedd Fair (John Thomas, 1870s)

marchnadfawr y mercher lafo o Ion, chwe. 13, maw. 21, mai 12, gor. 1, aw. 2, hyd 7, tach. 22. a nos Nadolig.

Ffeiriau SIR FEIRIONYDD, [*Merionethshire*].

ABERGYNOLWYN, mai 31, medi 15, hydref 16. *Aberdyfi*, awst 6 awst 6, hyd 20—*Bala*, sad Ynyd, iau cablyd, mai 11, mehefin dranoeth ff. y Ddinas, gor. 10, aw. 11, medi dran. ff. dinas, a'r 27, hyd. 24, tach. 8, rhag. 19 . . *Bettws*, maw 16, mehe. 22, aw. 12 medi16, rhag. 12. *Corwen*, Iau cyn y gwe. olaf o'r gauaf, maw 12 ebr 16, mai 21, meh. 30, aw. 19, hyd 6, rhag. 20. *Dinas Mowddy* gwe cyn sul blod. mehef. 2, medi 10, hyd. 18, tach 13—*Cynwyd*, aw 6, hyd. 21. *Dolgelleu* chwef 20, ebr. 21, mai 11, meh 27. aw 8 medi 20, hyd 9, tach 22, rhag 16—*Drwsnant*, medi 13, awst 9. *Ffestiniog*, maw 7, mai 24, meh 30, aw 15, medi 26 hyd. 23, tach 13 *Gwyddelwern*, ebr 15, awst 5, hyd. 18—*Harlech*, maw 4, ebr. 14, mai 13 aw 12, medi 22, tach. 10, rhag. 11—*Llandderfel*, aw 17 hyd 16. *Llandrillo*, chwe 25, mai 3, meh 29, ailiau yn gor. (gwlan aw 28, tach 14. *Llanfachreth*, medi 8 . *Llanddwywe*, mai 12 tach 9—*Llan-y-mawddwy*, iau lafyn maw, hyd 18. *Llanuwch-lyn* ebr 25, meh 20, medi 22, tach. 23—*Maentwrog*, maw 3, ebr 14 aw. 15, tach 10. . *Penrhyndeudraeth*, medi 2, aw. 10, medi 19, tach. 2 . *Llanbedr*, gwe. lafyn chwef. . *Trawsfynydd*, ebr 20 awst 7, medi 19 —*Towyn*, Llun Pasg, mai 14, medi 17.

Ffeiriau Sir DREFALDWYN, [*Montgomeryshire*].

BERIEW, ebr. 8, hyd. 14—*Caersws*, maw. 25, mehef. 24 hyd 14 *Cemmaes* sad . . .

black cattle in Haverfordwest; walked them to Whitland and Carmarthen, buying at each stop. They would carry on buying all the way to the English border and be accompanied all the way by a smith to shoe the newly bought beasts to protect their feet for the journey ahead. Another smith who accompanied droves to England was Robin y Go' (*Robin the smith*) of Penstryd, Trawsfynydd an immensely strong man who had command of five languages.[26] Sometimes when Robin was away, his wife would do the shoeing.

The types of animals

The animals walked to England by the drovers before the coming of the railways would have been quite different to today's highly improved stock. Apart from the quality, form and the age at which they were sold, major differences would have been found due to the natural variation in the stock of those days, mainly in their size, colour and fitness, especially among the cattle.

The cattle would have been store animals in which their hardiness was paramount. They had to thrive on fairly rough and exposed mountain pastures and be fit and strong enough to take the long journey to distant English markets.

On the better lands the cattle would have been larger than those of the mountain. The big horned and long bodied black Pembrokeshire cattle, especially the Castle Martin type were much favoured, as were those of Anglesey, Llŷn, Dyffryn Clwyd, Glamorgan and the Welsh borders. In his book, *Cattle* (1832), William Youatt refers to a market for the large strong Anglesey type as plough-oxen in Sussex.

They would be bought there from drovers as 3-4 year-olds and worked for a number of years as draft beasts before being sold on to local dealers to be driven to Smithfield in London.

The mountain cattle would have been small and very hardy and in the south-east of England two centuries ago, due to their small size, would have been referred to as 'Welsh Runts'. These were popular in that area and in the Romney Marshes at that time because for their size they would improve and put on weight better than practically any other type of cattle. Another factor was that the quality of the meat of mountain animals, whether cattle or sheep, was superior to that of lowland beasts. An important venue for Welsh drovers in the 18th century was the Michaelmas Runt Fair, October 6th-7th in Maidstone, Kent.

A great variation was found in cattle colour: predominantly black but there were many which were red, blue roan, grey, speckled, white, belted and line-backed. In Llŷn, grey cattle were common, as were white-faced in mid-Wales and red cattle with a white stripe down their back (line-backed) in Glamorgan.[27]

In the 1870s, when a pedigree herd book was opened for the Welsh breed or type, the predominant black colour was chosen as a defining feature for the new Welsh Black Cattle breed and many of the variations were gradually weeded out. Some, however, have been preserved by Gwartheg Hynafol Cymru (The Ancient Cattle of Wales Society) and developed as breeds in their own right.

The Welsh Black Cattle Society was among a number of pedigree societies to be formed in the British Isles during that period. As mentioned before there was no reason for this to happen until the right conditions prevailed. Those conditions were met when the rail network was established, allowing animals in an improved condition to be speedily transported to market.

Sheep were also taken to England by drovers but not to the same extent as cattle. The problem tended to be that mountain sheep can only be kept in certain areas. They were so small and nimble that no hedge or wall would keep them from escaping to raid surrounding

Cattle types from W Youat's 'Cattle' (1834):
1. Anglesey; 2. Pembroke; 3. Glamorgan

croplands. Their favoured destinations therefore were estate lands with high walls; lands claimed from the sea, such as the Essex flats, or drained areas such as the Romney Marshes. Here, where the field boundaries are ditches rather than hedges, and are wide enough to prevent the sheep from jumping across, is where these lively animals could be contained and managed.

An interesting story which illustrates this and is recorded by W Youatt in his book: *Sheep*[28] describes how a farmer from Mynydd Du in the west of the Brecon Beacons would drive sheep to be sold in Herefordshire. He was surprised to find that a few weeks later, one of these sheep re-appeared on her old mountain pasture. The following year he took her again, only for her to turn up again, and again the year after that. That sheep became quite a celebrity and quite profitable, having been sold by the farmer three times.

Modern Welsh Black cow with calf

Preparing to set off

Before setting off, the animals would sometimes have been bought over a few weeks or months prior to the journey and kept on the drover's farm until the market was at its best. This had the advantage of allowing the animals to familiarise and, following some butting and shoving, to sort out their hierarchy. Thus, when they eventually set off, the strongest or most dominant animal would take the lead, followed by others in descending order of rank to the least dominant at the back.

The main droving periods therefore corresponded with demand in the English grazing counties for store cattle either to fatten on pasture in the late spring and summer or for feeding on roots, hay or straw over the winter months.

The starting point would either be the drover's home farm or a gathering point where the cattle would be shod to protect their feet on the long journey (see below). Sheep would not have been shod and would have formed larger droves. They were frequently kept by the farmers who had sold them until their departure. For example Robert Jones of Abercin, Llanystumdwy in the 1820s regularly hired a field at nearby Tyddyn Sianel to start from. It was from here in September 1827 that he set off with 1,057 sheep and sold 1,056 of them in Pinner. The missing animal had become lame en route and had been sold.

Tyddyn Sianel

Shoeing cattle and geese

At the beginning of their long journey the cattle would have been shod with a pair of iron shoes or clips on each foot. This would protect their feet on some of the rocky tracks and hard roads they would encounter on their journey.

An interesting description of how cattle from Llŷn, coming through Llan Ffestiniog, were felled for shoeing is to be found in *Hanes Plwyf Ffestiniog* (1882), by GJ Williams:

"*A man tightly held the animal's nostrils with his left hand, and with his right hand he held the right hand horn; at the same time he would place his right heel tightly around the animal's front right foot; when ready to fell, he would gather all his strength, and while pulling the horn down, he would push the muzzle up; and while keeping his heel in place would throw the animal over on it's right side; in the fall the horn would generally sink into the ground; in this situation the animal would be kept by the man lying on its neck. The smith would now bind the feet together; after this a pole six or seven foot in length would be placed between the feet and belly; one end secure in the ground, and the other held by a third person; then would begin the shoeing, which would be done by securing two small iron 'clips' beneath each hoof. Felling an oxen was regarded as a feat calling for strength, bravery and nimbleness; the men best at fulfilling this task would be proud of themselves and would be looked up to by others.*"

A similar scene was described by a traveller visiting Dolgellau in 1865, who noted a large and noisy crowd in a circle on 'Y Marian' in the vicinity of the town's car park today. On closer inspection he found that they were observing and cheering cattle-shoeing. The smith and two helpers had come that morning from Llanuwchllyn to do the job and when an

1. Cattle shoes; 2. Tudor Beech, Llandegla holding an iron-tipped cattle shoeing pole; 3. Ifan Hughes preparing to shoe two Hereford oxen, part of Atora promotion, 1929

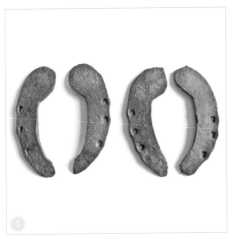

animal was brought into the ring betting would occur about how quickly the beast could be felled and shod. A great shout was heard when the animal was felled and coins thrown into the ring so that the men would earn some extra coppers in addition to the shilling a beast that they shared as payment for their work – the smith, who also provided and applied the iron clips, receiving sixpence while the feller and his helper received threepence each.

Two years later the railway arrived in Dolgellau, thus doing away with the need for shoeing cattle. Maybe the last example of such work in north-west Wales was in

1929 when, as part of a promotion by the Atora Beef Suet Company, a colourful covered waggon toured the countryside, pulled by two large Hereford oxen. A waggon and oxen was the company's logo and if you bought a suet packet which had the correct token on it you could take it to the waggon to be redeemed for a free packet of suet. A very imaginative promotion but when the oxen visited Pwllheli their hooves were worn. This is when Ifan Hughes the smith at Efailnewydd stepped in and shod the beasts. He knew exactly what to do as his father had shod cattle over sixty years previously.[29]

Geese would have also needed to be shod, or rather to have their feet protected for the journey. This would be done by walking the birds through warm pitch, then onto sand or fine gravel and finally through cold water which would harden the pitch. This would need to be repeated several times on the journey, depending on the nature of the terrain.

Geese needed to be handled with care and being slower they could only be moved 5-6 miles per day. The journey to

1. Humorous depiction of 'shoeing the goose', Beverley Minster; 2. Flock of geese being driven near King's Lynn

1. A frame or 'Chantier' for shoeing oxen in the Dordogne district in France; 2. Cattle frame in use, S France, 1980s

the English Midlands therefore would take months rather than weeks to complete. Apparently, the sound of flocks of geese being driven through the villages on their route was quite unique: the cackling of the birds themselves coupled with the pit-patting of hundreds of pitched feet on the cobbled roads. That sound is now long lost, only the folk-memory survives.

In the early 19th century goose-drovers would take flocks of the birds from Aberdaron near the tip of the Llŷn peninsula and from Penmachno in Dyffryn Conwy to England. In both these instances the men were cripples which meant that despite the disabilities which made it difficult for them to tackle hard manual work, they could easily manage walking their geese.

An interesting story dating from the turn of the 20th century tells of a farmer near Welshpool who, like many others in the vicinity, would rear a flock of geese to be sold in early December each year to Birmingham dealers. The birds would be loaded onto trucks at Welshpool station to be transported out.

This particular year the farmer had obtained a consignment of spent barley from a brewery in the town in order to fatten and finish the birds nicely for the sale. Unfortunately there was some residual alcohol in the barley and the birds became quite drunk and overexcited; cackling noisily and running across the field trying to fly. There was now a danger that they would lose condition, so the farmer had to quickly round them up and close them in a dark outbuilding to sober up. He never again fed his geese brewed barley.

Sheep, being fairly lightweight, did not require shoeing, nor usually did pigs. Pigs needed to be sold in good condition and are not very amenable to be driven far. Many were taken from the Llŷn peninsula on small ships directly to Liverpool where they would be killed near the docks and the meat salted in barrels to be taken by merchant shipping. Pigs could be taken by canal, overland in waggons, and if walking was required there are rare examples of small leather shoes, to be tied above the leg joint. One such example is housed at the Welsh Folk Museum, Sain Ffagans.

One of the seven inns once located around the drovers' smithy in the village of Ro-wen in the lower Conwy valley

Drivers and helpers

The drover would be responsible for the necessary arrangements as the journey proceeded and would need the assistance of a number of helpers or cattle 'drivers' as they were sometimes called. Some of these men would be regular and experienced hands employed on an annual basis for farm and droving work and would sometimes stay with that drover's family for most if not all of their working lives. The drover's son or sons would also help out, which would be a useful apprenticeship for when they took over. Other men might be occasional helpers taken on for an individual drove.

The sizes of droves could vary, usually 80-120 cattle from north-west Wales, with 3-4 men in attendance, but often larger from the south-western counties: droves of 100 to 400 attended by 4-8 men and their dogs. However, Rhys Morgan of Tregaron, styled 'King of Northampton', normally employed a dozen men to handle droves of up to 300 beasts.[30]

Some would be 'men of the road' or tramps, well used to living rough and would sleep in a barn or shed on the edge of the field where the cattle were kept at night. This would have been necessary for security as there were examples of cattle disappearing overnight. One such misfortune befell a farmer from Penychain near Pwllheli who, while driving 40 of his own and some neighbours' cattle to London in 1840, mysteriously lost them at night a few miles over the English border. Despite alerting the authorities, those cattle were never seen again. The farmer

'Two Cardiganshire drovers in Montgomery' (John Thomas, 1870s)

had to return home empty handed while a young girl, Ann Roberts, accompanying them to London had to find another drove to complete her journey. She needed to have a word with the son of the mansion-house of Broom Hall near Pwllheli who was in London at the time. The lady who told the author this story in 1988, a descendant of Ann, was proud of the aristocratic blood in her pedigree, albeit unofficial.

The 'men of the road' helping the drovers would receive food and drink on the journey and would be paid about a shilling a day, but would not receive full payment until the cattle had been sold. Few would use their earnings wisely, but rather would blow the lot on drink and the other delights that a town had to offer before returning to possibly accompany another drove.

Some of the experienced hands were contract drovers well able to manage the journey on their own. Robert Jones of Llanystumdwy in 1832 accompanied a drove as far as Ysbyty Ifan in Dyffryn Conwy before taking a stagecoach to Wrexham to arrange sales; the drove being left in the hands of an experienced employee for the rest of the journey. The Jonathans of Dihewyd frequently took large droves of cattle, over 200 beasts, and would frequently split them up towards the latter part of their journey for ease of passage and to avoid flooding their own market. Their regular hands would take charge of particular sections of the drove in such cases.

For certain parts of the journey extra help might be required. When starting out, the beasts would be in a state of excitement and would tend to start off at a trot before settling down to a regular pace after a day or two. Young boys would often accompany the drove to provide extra help for the first day or so and even to take an animal back if it showed lameness or any other condition that might slow it down. We find several possible references to this practice in drovers' accounts, e.g. on the second day of a drove from Tregaron to Chelmsford by the Jonathan family in October 1839, we find: "Boy drive the beast 2s (shillings)".

More help would be required when crossing estuaries, rivers and even the sea. "Guide across the sands, 1/-" is occasionally seen in accounts of crossing the treacherous quicksand of the Glaslyn estuary, before the land was claimed from

Caban Twm Bach near the Wye crossing

the sea following the completion of the Cob at Porthmadog in 1812.

Ferries would be used for crossing rivers when the nearest bridge was too distant. A dramatic and tragic event occurred in 1815 when cattle were being ferried across the Wye at Erwyd. The ferry was being pulled across the river attached to a rope by Twm Bach and his son. Unfortunately the river was in flood and the boat turned on its side, sweeping all away. The two ferrymen were drowned but the drovers and their cattle survived, the drovers having clung to the tails of their beasts to gain land.[31]

Crossing the Menai Srait from Anglesey could sometimes be quite challenging before the Telford's Suspension Bridge was completed in 1827. Sheep, pigs and geese would be transported across on boats – yes, even the geese, since they would be masters of their own element and difficult to control on the open water. Cattle would be swum across at slack water either from Beaumaris at low tide or from Porthaethwy, below the bridge at low or high tide. Experienced boatmen would accompany them, having tied a rope to the horns of the lead steer which would be rowed across, with the others following.

Cattle are excellent swimmers and when a Dublin-Holyhead cattle boat was sunk by a U-boat in 1915, the captain, Watkin Williams of Edern, was saved by climbing onto the back of one of the cattle to await rescue. He earned the nickname 'Capten buwch' (Captain cow) as a result.

When unable to bypass some towns and villages local help would be appreciated and at fairs at the far end. References frequently occur in droving accounts to, for example: "For hands to keep the cattle together at Epping and Coldhill, 6/-"[32], "Men at Rugby Fair 3/6"[33].

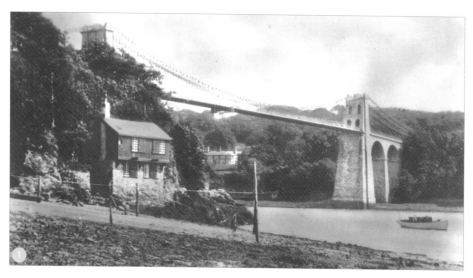

1. Pont Menai – the cattle would swim across and land near the base of the column in the distance; 2. Swimming from Skye to the mainland, the cattle stick together in a tight bunch; 3. Old ford to cross the Wye after leaving Mynydd Epynt

On the trail of the Welsh Drovers

Dogs

In addition to human helpers dogs would be essential to control the animals. The corgi was reputedly developed by drovers from south-west Wales especially for the work. They are lively, tireless, plucky and ready to get in close to nip the heel of a slow beast. Being so short, the corgi is low enough to avoid the back-kick which invariably follows their attention. A cattle dog like the corgi would not be favoured for driving sheep since under no circumstance should the dog's teeth touch the animal.

North Wales drovers used larger dogs. These would be strong, powerful animals, frequently red in colour and ready on command to defend their master against thieves. Several stories have survived about such encounters, for example that of the dog 'Dermyd Lwyd' of Neigwl in Llŷn. This big grey dog became separated from his master in Barnett Fair near London and the drover had to return home alone with the sales money. That night, he stayed at an Inn and had been given a back-room on the ground floor.

Having gone to sleep, he was woken up by a noise outside and was very surprised to find that it was Dermyd Lwyd. He pulled the dog in through the window and eventually, after the excitement of their reunion, both went to sleep, with the dog lying on the bed. Later the drover was again woken by the dog, this time growling. He sat up and put his hand on the animal to quieten it. He then realised that Dermyd Lwyd was responding to a floorboard gently creaking outside. Then,

A red coloured Welsh sheepdog, commonly employed for driving cattle and sheep

the latch of the door slowly opened and somebody, in the darkness, crept into the room towards the bed. The drover shouted *"Cydia fo Dermyd Lwyd!!"* – the command to attack – and the dog leapt forward in the darkness! Such were the intruder's screams and barking of the dog that the whole house was roused and soon people poured in with lamps. The drover pulled the dog off the flailing, bloody body on the floor to reveal that it was the tavern-keeper and beside him, a knife.

In the morning the Constables were called and eventually, upon interrogation, the would-be assailant admitted having murdered several people for their money while they slept in that back-room. He was hung, whereas Dermyd Lwyd became a hero.[34]

Stories from Dyffryn Clwyd and Harlech tell of how some of the dogs would find their own way home from England. Usually the dogs of hired hands, they followed the route by which they had come and received a crust to eat at some of the taverns at which they had stayed. When the dogs arrived home the wives knew that the men would be home in four or five days.

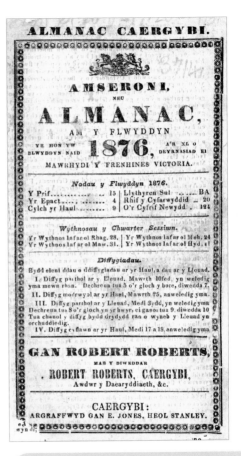

Almanac Caergybi 1876, an essential listing of Welsh fairs

On the road

A drove of animals on their journey would have been quite a sight: the animals proceeding in an orderly fashion; hired hands and dogs on foot while the head drover usually rode on horseback.

One of the men would have gone at least half a mile ahead to make sure there were no obstacles in their way, no gaps or open gates and to ensure the beasts went the right way if there was a fork in the road. A feature of an approaching drove, especially through more populated areas of countryside would be the noise; the cattle lowing; dogs barking and the men shouting or half-yodelling: "Haip! Trrrrrrrw-how!" This would be an obvious warning to all in the district to move any loose animals out of the way in case they inadvertently joined the drove and be taken away. The drovers might not always stop and waste time to remove such interlopers.

According to Professor EG Bowen of Aberystwyth who interviewed men who had walked cattle to England, drovers and cattle drivers frequently wore wide-brimmed hats, a smock and long coat, knee-length woollen socks and clogs. Wax-paper would be wound around the body between the clothes and around the legs to prevent rain and cold from penetrating directly to the skin. Soap would be rubbed onto the soles of the socks to prevent blistering. This would not be the purified and scented soap we use today but coarser soft soap which contained excess sheep grease, rich in lanolin. Lanolin is the active ingredient of many of our modern skin-care products.

Most men would carry a long thin stick which would make an appropriate 'wooooosh' to drive the cattle forward while the head drover frequently carried a shorter stick with a blade inside it or a stout ash stick to protect himself against thieves.

After a day or two on the road the cattle would have settled to the routine of the journey and would follow the lead beast in a line of descending rank or dominance without much trouble. Similarly, sheep would quickly learn the routine and would often follow the man up ahead. Once that routine had been established it was important to proceed in an orderly fashion to reach their destination in a reasonable time – not too quickly to avoid lameness and loss of condition, and not too slowly because there were target dates to achieve. For example the Maidstone Fair, October 6th-7th, was an important venue for north Wales drovers in the 18th century. Their aim was to arrive on the 5th to allow the animals some rest; it would be no good to arrive on the 8th.

Since the main droving period during the year would have been the late summer and autumn, there was always a chance of bad weather. This is a consequence of the equinoxial gales characteristic of this time of year, which frequently are the tail-ends of hurricanes which sweep up along the eastern US seaboard and across the north Atlantic to us. Luckily these storms will have lost most of their power by the time they reach us, but can make travelling rather cold and unpleasant. Having started in good weather, if a storm arrived there was no stopping for a few days to let it pass – the mileage had to be maintained.

During the day and in the evening the drover would pay for food and drink for his helpers. But while the drover himself slept in the tavern the men would be obliged to sleep out with the animals to keep an eye on them, or in a barn by the field if they were lucky. Poor accommodation and bad weather on the road would sometimes take their toll on drovers' helpers and there are instances in Church records in the south of England of 'poor droving man', with no other means of identification, being found dead in a barn and buried in an unmarked pauper's grave.[35]

The aim was to cover an average of 12-14 miles a day, depending on the weather and ground conditions. They would move off at dawn at the animals' own fairly steady pace covering about two or three miles an hour, allowing the animals to graze as they moved. They tended to stop awhile if good grazing or clean drinking water was available. The drover's art was to get the beasts to the far end in good condition, even better than when they started off. This was achievable since, given sufficient pasture en route, the physical exertion of walking for two or three weeks would make the animals fairly muscular and in good condition.

The men as well as the beasts required occasional watering as described in a story

from Dyffryn Conwy of a flock of sheep being driven to Rhuthun. By arrangement with the others one of the men up ahead ordered drinks from a roadside tavern. The landlord duly brought beer on a tray to the door so the men could down their pints and pay without having to delay the progress of the flock.

1. Set of drover's horn drinking cups and snuff box from Trawsfynydd. The cups fit into each other for ease of carrying; 2. Water troughs at Llangollen; the lower one is for the dogs; 3. The famous Drovers Arms on Mynydd Epynt; 4. Rhydspence tavern

On the trail of the Welsh Drovers

Tracks, roads and tollgates

In the mid-18th century, in order to improve the poor condition of the road system, licences were issued to private consortia or Turnpike Trusts to repair and maintain specific stretches of roadway, for which they could then charge road users. For the next century and more tollhouses became a regular feature of the most well used roadways. This sometimes lead to friction as witnessed by the Rebecca riots of the 1840s when scores of tollgates were smashed in mid and south-west Wales as part of an organised popular reaction against their oppressive costs.

While crossing the Welsh uplands the drovers could easily avoid having to use toll roads, using instead the ancient network of strategic tracks over the *bylchau* (gaps) as they headed from west to east. Welsh cattle and sheep reared on hill and mountain pastures would have no problem with this high terrain and the tracks over the unenclosed mountains would often be far more direct and quicker than the circuitous routes around the more populated mountain bases.

Land in lower areas however would have been enclosed by hedges and field walls making it difficult to avoid having to use the roads. If unimproved tracks could be found, all well and good, but frequently there would be no choice other than toll roads for particular sections of the journey. It is interesting to note that the Jonathans of Dihewyd, taking droves of cattle from Tregaron to Pinner in the 1830s were able to avoid the extra overhead costs of road tolls all the way across Wales. But once they hit the English border, tolls of 15-18 shillings had to be paid at least once a day. Toll rates were usually 1/- per score (20 beasts) for cattle and 6d per score for sheep or pigs.

Ingenious methods would sometimes be employed to reduce costs. Approaching a tollgate, two men would mount the drover's horse, sheep would be carried over men's shoulders, a goose under each arm, because payment could not be extracted for those whose feet did not

1. & 2. Tollbridge at Witney-on-Wye with prices; 3. & 4. Llanfair Gate and prices, Llanfairpwllgwyngyll, Anglesey

Anno Domini 1796

Tolls Vested by Act of Parliament
Twelfth Day of July

	The Sum of
For every horse, mare, gelding, ox, or other beast drawing any carriage	4½d
For every horse, mare, gelding, laden, unladen, and not drawing	2½d
For every person on foot, passenger	1d
For every score of oxen, cows or neat cattle	10d
- and so in proportion for any greater or less number -	
And for every score of calves, hogs, sheep or lambs	5d
- and so in proportion for any greater or less number -	

Tolls to be taken at
LLANFAIR GATE.

	s.	d.
For every Horse, Mule, or other Cattle, drawing any Coach, or other Carriage, with springs the sum of		4
For every Horse, Mule or other Beast or Cattle drawing any Waggon, Cart, or other such Carriage, not employed solely in carrying or going empty to fetch Lime for manure the sum of		3
For every Horse, Mule, or other Beast or Cattle, drawing any Waggon, Cart, or other such Carriage, employed solely in carrying or going empty to fetch Lime for manure the sum of		1½
For every Horse, Mule or Ass laden or unladen, and not drawing, the sum of		1
For every Drove of Oxen, Cows, or other neat Cattle per score, the sum of		10
For every Drove of Calves, Sheep, Lambs, or Pigs per score, the sum of		5

For every Horse, Mule or other beast drawing any Waggon, or Cart the Wheels being less than 3 inches breadth, or having Wheels with Tires fastened with Nails projecting and not countersunk to pay double Toll

A Ticket taken here clears Carnedd Du Bar.

touch the ground. Even ten years after the building of the Menai Bridge, travellers crossing by coach to Holyhead in 1837 reported seeing cattle being swum across the Strait below them. Thus, despite the convenience of the bridge, a toll was payable and Anglesey drovers if they could get away with it preferred not to pay a toll at all.

Having to use toll roads would not have been all bad. The roads would have been direct, well maintained, with good boundaries and wide enough to allow oncoming traffic to pass. Toll roads would be surfaced with packed stone, with a lengthman responsible for particular sections of road and would fill in potholes. In the early part of the droving season good grazing was available on the verges and, if need be, the cattle could be kept overnight on the side of the road which would reduce the cost of overnight pasturage. An indication of the droving traffic is given by the novelist Daniel Defoe who records that during a journey from Gloucester to Cardiff in the 1740s, his coach stopped 14 times to allow droves of cattle to pass.

The drovers were not always popular with other road users. They may not have caused much of a problem along upland tracks, but when it came to enclosed routes and roadways through lower areas, things could sometimes be different. Who indeed would appreciate having to stop frequently to allow droves to pass or have to follow slowly behind a drove on unmade tracks which, in wet weather, would be very much churned by the cattle's hooves and very mucky.

Daniel Defoe refers, humorously no doubt, to walking on an unmade track on heavy Oxford clay; jumping or clod-hopping from one dry bit of turf to another. Seeing a hat lying on the mud ahead, he kicked it. "Awww!" A pained scream emanated from below the hat from the head of a man who had sunk almost to his nostrils. Defoe apologised profusely, saying he had not realised that there was anybody there and helped to liberate the man from his muddy prison. "Thank you", said the man before asking Defoe for one more favour: "Could you now please help me to get my horse out."

Stagecoach drivers were not enamoured by drovers on the road. Having

Mailcoach, transferring mail without stopping

to slow down or even stop to allow animals to pass several times a day was considered a nuisance especially for mail-coaches, which wanted to travel quickly. The rough appearance of droving men was also viewed with suspicion as they could easily be highwaymen.

The drovers in turn were not amused by the coachmen's haughty attitude. A story recorded by Will Ellis, a drover from Penmachno[36] illustrates how the relationship between them could easily turn quite sour. Will was bringing a drove up a winding road when the man up ahead saw a coach approaching and tried to wave it down to warn of the cattle just around the corner. The coachman, thinking that the man was a robber, whipped his horses to greater speed, lashed at the 'thief' in passing and drove his coach with vigour around the corner, ploughing into the cattle and causing a great commotion. As the coach drove off, Will, livid with anger, ran across the field to intercept the coach after the next bend; yanked a large piece of wood from the hedge and thrust it into the wheel of the passing vehicle. This caused it to swerve and capsize, spilling the driver and passengers onto the road verge 'cackling like noisy geese'. Having committed an illegal act, Will now ran back to his drove and moved quickly away. He was very proud of how he'd got his revenge on that coachman.

Overnight stops

The drovers would aim for a particular tavern to stay overnight, one which would have a field attached to secure the animals. But if their preferred stop was already taken there would be others available, or even a convenient farm which could put them up. Place-names sometimes refer to these overnight stops: Llety Lloegr (meaning a stopover on the road to England) in Ardudwy while well over a dozen Drovers Arms for pubs past and present survive on some of the major drove routes across Wales. The Drovers House, in the village of Stockbridge on the South Downs still retains a welcoming advert to drovers from south Wales on their way to Kent: '*Gwair tymherus, porfa flasus, cwrw da, gwal gysurus*' (quality hay, tasty pasture, good beer, comfortable bed).

A few field-names refer to Cae Cardis (Cardiganshire men's field), Gwaun Drofer (drover's moor) and Pantyporthmon (hollow of the drover) in Dyfed, while Halfpenny Field is not uncommon along drove roads in England, referring to the payment per head per night for cattle. Welsh Road is a name which is frequently

found, referring to stretches of old drove roads in central and southern England.[37]

Dafydd Jones of Caeo, the drover and hymnwriter, even named his home Llundain Fechan (little London), while many marts were and still are refered to as Smithfield. At Foel, Montgomeryshire, where cattle were shod at the Glan yr Afon Inn, we find two small fields: Cae Caint (Kent field) and Cae Essex (Essex field), named for the destinations of the cattle

1. *The Drovers House Stockbridge;*
2. *Well at Stockbridge for cattle and sheep;*
3. *Tafarn Bara Ceirch, Llangernyw*

inflated to cover the price of the 'free' drink.

Common land was another option and would be sought by some drovers who would aim to arrive there on a Saturday afternoon. They would stay until Monday morning because fines would be imposed in some counties for walking animals on the Sabbath. For example, in 1817, two Welsh drovers were convicted for "... *profanation of the Sabbath in driving cattle through the village of Mordiford in Herefordshire.*"[38] Some tollgates would charge double on that day.

It was the convenience of a large tract of common land which accounted for the importance of Llandegla near Wrexham for the drovers. Droves could graze overnight for free on the common and many would aim to arrive on the Saturday evening to stay until the Monday morning. There were over 20 taverns in that small village willing to accommodate drovers including Tafarn y Gath, kept in the 1850s-60s by an interesting and humorous character, William Jones, better known by his poetic name, Ehedydd Iâl. He would hold regular eisteddfodau (competitions for singing and poetry) in the tavern – the

shod there. There is a Cae Pedloi (shoeing field) near Llanbadarn Fawr, Aberystwyth and Pedolfa (shoeing place) on the edge of the Elenydd in Ceredigion.

An interesting place-name, Tafarn Bara Ceirch (*oatbread tavern*), on the old road above Llangernyw from Llanrwst to Abergele refers to premises not licensed to sell alcohol. Drovers and travellers bought oatbread to eat and got a free pint with it. The price of the oatbread was deliberately

1. Plaque to Ehedydd Iâl; 2. Tafarn y Gath; 3. Tafarn Cwm Owen; 4. Drover's statue, Llanymddyfri; 5. Ysbyty Ifan

prizes invariably being more beer – and religious discussions on the Sunday.

Some farms and smallholdings would be happy to accommodate the drover's cattle, not only for the payment they received but also for the good job of manuring the field. As the winter approached it became more difficult to find good pasture as, especially towards the end of the journey, the hooves of previous droves had poached the ground where the traffic in animals increased as their routes converged. This, along with a bid to improve the condition of the beasts for the approaching sales may explain increasingly frequent payments for hay towards the end of the drove.

A frequent sign that a tavern or farmhouse would welcome drovers and their animals would be three Scots pines planted nearby. Being evergreen these conifers would stand out and be visible for miles. They would also signal to the more sedate travellers that rough and lively drovers would share accommodation with them and that there would be a field-full of animals outside. Three pines would also be planted on open moorland to show the right direction and often with a stone wall around their base as protection when the trees were young.

There would be revelry when drovers stayed at particular taverns. Some of the men would challenge local farmhands to wrestling matches or, as in the village of Ysbyty Ifan, a local champion would challenge the drovers. The experience of some men in felling cattle for shoeing would now prove very useful. A crowd of people would gather and there would be much encouragement and betting on the outcomes. The winners could earn extra shillings and beer.

Above: The Scotch Pine Tavern on Mynydd Betws above the Aman valley;
1. Pine trees at Blaen-y-cae, south of Trawsfynydd; 2. Pine trees near Llety Lloegr

Drovers' routes

The Welsh countryside abounds in drove routes, some of which are now under tarmac but many over the mountain passes survive for long distances almost in their original condition. Today these make wonderful linear walks, provided they haven't been rutted to destruction by trail-bikes and other motorised vehicles.

Before the coming of the railways, Welsh drove routes could be likened to a number of trees lying on their sides; their roots being in north and west Wales while their divergent branches would be in central and south-eastern England. The root tips correspond to the fairs and farms from where the animals started and, once on the road, would converge into ever-thickening root branches which would eventually merge into a number of main trunks before splitting towards the far end into increasingly finer branches, the tips of which end in the fairs scattered over the grazing counties where the animals would be sold.

Most Welsh drove routes would converge on certain strategic nodal points in the borderlands: Wrexham, Shrewsbury, Leebotswood, Ludlow, Leominster, Hereford, Monmouth and some of the ports in Glamorgan and Gwent to cross the Severn Estuary.[39] Sometimes these centres would be the end of the journey as the animals might be sold to fatten locally or to other drovers to be taken further. Pigs would frequently converge on the canal system in some border areas to be transported by barge to towns and cities.

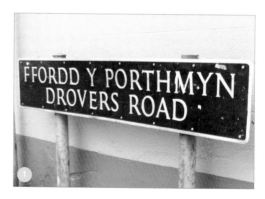

1. Lampeter;
2. Map of main drove roads in Wales

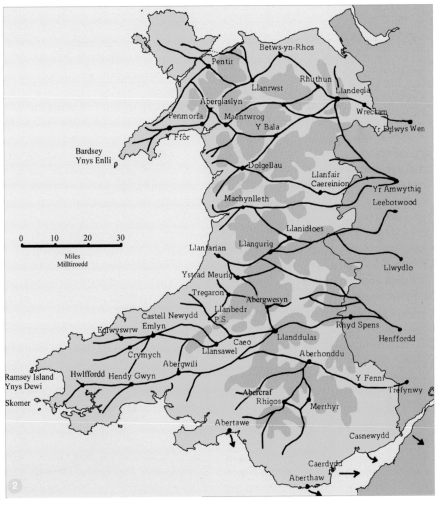

Drove routes to the Border area

From Anglesey – Before the completion of the Menai Bridge in 1827 the greatest obstacle for Anglesey drovers was the Menai Strait. Sheep, pigs and geese needed to be ferried across by boat while cattle would be obliged to swim across during the slack-water periods which occur for about 20-30 minutes at high and low tide. It would be hazardous to cross at other times since the tidal race between high and low tide would gradually increase to white-water force at mid-tide before slowing to slack-water again.

Cattle in water tend to stick together in a tight bunch and it would have been necessary to tie a rope around the horns of the lead animal and row it across with the others following. If the timing was not right the animals would have found a strengthening current on approaching the mainland side causing the ones at the front to veer to the side. There was a danger then that their noses would be diverted to the back of the bunch, causing the beasts to swim in a circle which would be almost impossible to break up. If not careful the strengthening current might

then sweep the whole drove along to more unfavourable landfalls some distance away either on the Anglesey or mainland side. If very unlucky the drove might even be split, with some landing on opposite shores.

The crossing points were either at Porthaethwy, landing near the foot of the suspension bridge, or from Gallows Point, Beaumaris, swimming the short distance across at low tide to the sands of Traeth Lafan and on to Abergwyngregyn.

Having crossed at Porthaethwy the droves would make their way to Pentir, where they would join the drove track originating through various branches from the vicinities of Caernarfon, Dyffryn Nantlle and through Clynnog from northern Llŷn. From Pentir the route took them along the old road up Nant Ffrancon to Capel Currig from where they went over the top, past Llyn Craflwyn to Llanrwst or proceed towards Betws y Coed.

1. Pont Menai with tollbooth; 2. Traeth Lafan; 3. Bwlch Sychnant; 4. From Capel Currig to Craflwyn and Llanrwst

If there was a sea mist while crossing the expansive sands of Traeth Lafan the church bells at Abergwyngregyn would be rung to guide drovers and travellers in the right direction. From here they would follow the ancient trackway over Bwlch y Ddeufaen to the Conwy valley and down to Llanrwst which was the most convenient site to cross the River Conwy before Telford's bridge at Conwy was erected in 1826.

From Llanrwst the drovers could head towards Rhuthun, Llandegla and out to England via Wrexham or Oswestry. Alternatively they would head through Llangernyw to Abergele where the beasts could be sold on to other drovers who would take them on to England, while the Anglesey men returned home to bring another drove.

Ynys Môn or Anglesey has always been famous for its *moch Môn* (Anglesey pigs) and in 1840 a steamer service, on the good ship Eyre, took pigs and passengers from Porthdinllaen on the northern side of Llŷn, calling by Caernarfon, Bangor and Beaumaris. The pigs would be taken to Liverpool docks to be converted into salted pork in barrels for shipping.

From Llŷn – Animals from Llŷn and Eifionydd would head towards Penmorfa on the edge of the Glaslyn estuary. They usually would have taken the back-roads, skirting and avoiding towns like Pwllheli and Cricieth; the Llŷn men probably calling by the famous Tafarn Gorniog (corniog = horns) near Llannor.

Penmorfa was frequently an overnight stop, depending on the condition of the estuary. The tide, which at its highest would have reached Aberglaslyn over four miles inland, would need to have been out and with no flood in the river for a safe crossing. This crossing, from Prenteg to Llanfrothen was hazardous because of quicksand and the services of a "guide to cross the sands, 1/-" features in some accounts. Once safely across they would rest at Maes Gwŷr Llŷn (field of the men of Llŷn)

Droves from slightly further north would have come through Dolbenmaen and over the top to Prenteg past the gatehouse and tavern of Tŷ Newydd,

1. Tafarn Gorniog; 2. Penamser to await a favourable tide to cross Traeth Mawr; 3. & 4. The old Aberglaslyn to Croesor road

locally known as Gatws Uffern (gatehouse to hell) because of the reputation of the old lady who kept it of getting drovers drunk and relieving them of their money.

If the tide and river flooding made it impossible to cross, then an alternative route, involving circumventing the estuary was called for. Drovers at Dolbenmaen would have been made aware of this and would cross to Cwm Ystradllyn and over Bwlch Oerddwr to Beddgelert, a mile upstream from the bridge at Aberglaslyn. Droves from Llŷn arriving at Penmorfa could either follow the edge of the estuary if conditions allowed it or make their way to Cwm Ystradllyn.

From Aberglaslyn the droves would follow the ancient route-way / coach-road to Bwlch Gwernog and up the wonderful old trackway to Croesor and on over the top to Tan y Bwlch in Dyffryn Maentwrog. This diversion became unnecessary when the Cob was completed by William Maddocks in 1812 to claim the estuary for agriculture.

The drovers would aim to stop overnight in the vicinity of Llan Ffestiniog because the following day would involve the long and arduous crossing of the Migneint moor. They would either pass Ffynnon Eidda, with its *Ŷf a bydd Ddiolchgar* (drink and be thankful) inscription and on to Ysbyty Ifan, Cerrigydrudion, Rhuthun and Llandegla, or cross to Bala and on to Shrewsbury.

From Ardudwy

From the west coast the droves would cross the spine of the Rhinogydd through the strategic gaps of Bwlch Tyddiad, following the Medieval pack-horse trail erroneously known as the Roman Steps, and Bwlch Drws Ardudwy (the doorway to Ardudwy) towards Bronaber and eventually Bala. South of these is the old coach-road from Harlech over the magnificent bridge, Pont Scethin, and climbing over Llawllech to Bontddu, joining the route from Llety Lloegr over the aptly named Bwlch y Rhiwgyr (gap of the slope of the drove). Crossing north of Harlech is another old track, over Bwlch y moch (gap of the pigs) to Trawsfynydd.

From Dolgellau the main drove route passes the Cross Foxes Inn which still

1. Milestone above Tan y Bwlch, Maentwrog; 2. Dyffryn Maentwrog; 3. Ffynnon Eidda; 4. Drovers Arms at Rhewl near Rhuthun

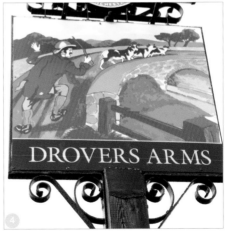

FFYNNON EIDDA
Yf a bydd Ddiolchgar

DROVERS ARMS

retains its pine trees indicative of a droving inn and over to Dinas Mawddwy, Llangadfan, y Trallwm (Welshpool) and Shrewsbury.

From Dysynni
North of Towyn and the rich Dysynni valley, branches of the Ffordd Ddu (the black road, due to the peaty nature of the ground) converge on Llyn Gregennan and on to Dolgellau. Further south, routes converge on Pennal before proceeding to Machynlleth.

From Machynlleth
Depending on the destination one could choose the northerly route through Dolgadfan and Talerddig, then along the old drove road known as Rhyd y biswail (ford of slurry, a very appropriate name for a drove route) to Llanllugan, Forden and along the Long Mountain to Shrewsbury.

Alternatively, one could follow the track through Dylife and Trefeglwys and head either towards and around Y Drenewydd (Newtown) and on to Y

1. .Pont Scethin; 2. Llety Lloegr; 3. The Cross Foxes with pine tree; 4. From the Cross Foxes over Bwlch Oerddwr to Dinas Mawddwy

Trallwm for Shrewsbury, or to Llandinam and over the Ceri hills for Bishop's Castle, the Long Mynd and Leebotswood. Otherwise, before reaching Y Drenewydd, one could head for Betws-y-crwyn in the Clun Forest and on to Ludlow.

From Northern Ceredigion
Through Ponterwyd for Llangurig and Y Drenewydd or from Llanilar and Pontrhydygroes to Llangurig or to Pontrhydfendigaid and over to Rhaeadr Gwy, Penybont and Kington on the way to Leominster or Hereford.

From Tregaron
Tregaron was an important focus for animals from central Ceredigion. From here went probably Wales' most famous drove road: over the hills to Abergwesyn, then over Cefn Cardis (ridge of the Cardiganshire men) to Beulah, Newbridge on Wye, Llandrindod and Kington.

Another route from Abergwesyn involved heading towards Llanwrtyd, Cwm Owen and Erwyd (Erwood). The river Wye had to be crossed just north of Erwyd and it was here by the Boat Inn, about two centuries ago, that the ferry overturned, drowning Twm Bach the ferry-man, while the drovers were saved because they clung on to the tails of their cattle and were pulled to safety. Having safely crossed the Wye the drovers took their beasts to Painscastle, Rhydspens and on to Hereford.

From Llanbed (**Lampeter**)

This was another important focus for drove routes converging from the west. From Llanbed the animals would be driven through Cilycwm and Caeo, then either through Talgarth over Mynydd Epynt past the famous Drovers Arms (now a ruin) to Erwyd or through Porthyrhyd to Llanymddyfri and Aberhonddu (Brecon). Many place-names testify to the drovers' passage: near Pumpsaint is a farm called Llundain Fechan (little London) where the famous hymn-writer Dafydd Jones of Caeo lived; Rhyd y Defaid (ford of the sheep); Rhyd yr Ychen (ford of the oxen) and Drovers Arms taverns at Llanbed, Farmers, Porthyrhyd and Cilycwm.

From northern Pembrokeshire

Drovers from Eglwyswrw, Crymych and further west would come to Castell Newydd Emlyn, from where they could head either to Llanbed or Llandysul. From Llandysul they would head eastwards over Mynydd Llanybydder to Rhydcymerau. It is interesting to note that this track is called Rhyd y Biswail on the western side of the mountain and Heol Lloegr (the road to England) as it comes to Rhydcymerau. Onwards to Llansawel to Porthyrhyd where they would join the droves coming from Llanbed on their way to Llanymddyfri.

From Hwlffordd (**Haverfordwest**)

From here they would head through Arberth and Hendygwyn (Whitland) where some of the droves would head north-east through Llanboidy and Henfeddau towards Castell Newydd Emlyn. Most though would go through Sainclêr, Caerfyrddin, Llandeilo towards Llanymddyfri and on to Aberhonddu (Brecon). Others would head eastwards through Castell Nedd (Neath) to Y Bontfaen (Cowbridge) in Bro Morgannwg (Vale of Glamorgan) to a number of

1. Tregaron to Abergwesyn road; 2. At Builth Wells; 3. Llundain Fechan; 4. Over Mynydd Llanybydder

crossing points on the Severn estuary as far as Gwent. This though would be a fairly tortuous route given the numerous rivers that needed to be crossed emanating from the heads of the valleys.

From Morgannwg and Gwent

Many animals would be taken across the Severn estuary from Swansea, Aberthaw, Cardiff or Newport while a major crossing point for sheep was from near the mouth of the Wye either by the ferry to Aust in Gloucestershire (near the Severn Bridge) or to Redwick near Bristol to access the routes eastwards along the South Downs. Thousands of sheep would be driven this way to the Romney Marshes in Kent.

Others, from eastern Glamorgan and Gwent would be driven through Trefynwy (Monmouth) to Gloucester. On the whole, from the mid to late 18th century, Glamorgan and Gwent progressively exported fewer and fewer animals compared with other areas of Wales because the rapidly increasing industrial populations of the south Wales valleys and Cardiff generated a market in their own right.

Many drovers preferred not to traverse the old county of Glamorgan and would instead, especially in the western areas, prefer to go north-east through Abercrâf or Rhigos, or north from Penybont (Bridgend) through Merthyr and over Bwlch Pen-y-fan to converge on Aberhonddu (Brecon). Here they would join the major arterial drove route coming from west Wales via Llanymddyfri. From Aberhonddu they could either head north-east to Llyswen, Rhydspens and on to Hereford or would proceed to Y Fenni (Abergavenny) and Trefynwy (Monmouth) to Gloucester and beyond.

1. *Llanymddyfri Rugby Club;*
2. *Drovers Arms, Aberhonddu;*
3. *Drovers Arms, Cefncoedcymerau;*
4. *Ruin of an old droving inn on the Grwyne Fawr track, Black Mountains*

Drove Roads and destinations in England

Whereas Smithfield Market in the heart of London was the ultimate destination for most of the animals, the main sales would have originally been to graziers, in the autumn, in a great ring of fairs around the city, e.g. Billericay, Brentwood, Harlow, Epping, the great 'Welsh Fair' at Barnet, Pinner, Uxbridge, Reigate, Maidstone, Canterbury and several more.[40] Here, farmers would buy cattle as store animals to be fattened over the winter on root crops and sold over the following months and into the spring, thus extending the supply of meat through the winter and early spring, since the drovers would not travel during that period.

As the population grew rapidly in the industrial Midlands from the mid to late 18th century onwards, Gloucester and Northamptonshire became increasingly important and would take most of the stock by the mid-19th century. Northampton was ideally and centrally located, with excellent pastureland for fattening, between London and the rapidly developing Midland towns.

By the late 19th century several Welsh drovers were renting or buying land in the area so that they could fatten and hang on to the beasts to await the best prices. Many families of Welsh descent still farm here today. Stories are told of how they would hire a train for their migration from west Wales, with the furniture in the first carriage, the family in the second and the stock and farm implements in the other carriages.

We can identify the fairs targeted by the Welsh drovers from their accounts. For example the most important fairs for the Jonathan family of Dihewyd between 1832 and 1889 were Northampton, Market Harborough, Gloucester, Rugby and Lutterworth. If the market was unfavourable here they would go on to the Home Counties to sell their beasts in Harlow, Chelmsford, Romford, Epping or Brentwood.

Crossing the river Tanat to Shropshire at Llanyblodwel with the Horseshoe Inn at the bridge's end

An old lady at Ingatestone in Essex remembered the fairs held there yearly on December the first at the end of the 19th century, when the fields around the village were covered by Welsh cattle before the fair and Welsh voices common on the street.[41] She remembered the rhyme:

Harlow fair and Ingatestone
Then the Welshman may go home.

References are found to the difficulty of selling in some years. In which case they would move from fair to fair seeking an

acceptable price which, invariably, would entail mounting costs. One example is John Williams, Drws y Nant, Rhydymain in the late 18th century.[42] He had brought 113 cattle from Bala to Billericey in Essex and moved to Brentwood, Epping and Coldhill. He only received £265-13-0 for the drove, out of which £47-17-3 in expenses needed to be subtracted.

Another example is found in a letter from John Roberts, Tŷ Cerrig of Ynys, near Harlech. He wrote from the Three Rabbits Inn, Mannor Park, east of London and half way to Romford, at Easter 1816, complaining bitterly about the weather and the difficulty of selling the 25 beasts remaining a week after he had sold the others. He advises his wife about the necessary work at home: *"gyrrwch ar drrin y ddauar heb ddisgwil dim wrtha i Rhowch ddarn o Gongl ucha Cau Penybryn i fytatws..."* (Carry on turning the land without expecting anything from me Plant potatoes in the upper corner of Penybryn field).[43]

A muddy farm track today but once a drove road used by Welsh drovers in Oxfordshire

Demands in the English Counties

The main targets for Welsh drovers in the 18th century were Kent and the Home Counties. Farmers in these areas fattened cattle for the enormous London market, buying them in the Autumn in a circle of fairs around the outskirts of the capital such as Billericay, Brentwood, Harlow, Epping, Barnet's great Welsh Fair, Pinner, Uxbridge, Reigate, Maidstone's famous 'Runt Fair' and Canterbury. Some of the Welsh black cattle came to Smithfield from the pastures of Wiltshire, while others would have been driven to the fairs of Blackwater, Farnborough and down to Horsham, East Grinstead and Brighton.

William Marshall in 1798 described how important Welsh cattle were in Kent:

"...there is not a region in the Island that breeds so few of its own stock. It might be said that more or less all its stock is Welsh... The cattle are brought here, mainly by Welsh drovers, when young; at one, two or three years of age. They come from different parts of the principality. But the heifers, for milking, are of the Pembroke type... In October the roads to everywhere are filled with them; some heading for the hills, others for the marshes."

A similar picture is presented by Youatt (1834), who indicates that there were far more Scottish cattle being bought by then:

"In the east of Kent especially, few cattle are bred. The polled Scots are bought for summer grazing, or the Welsh are purchased at Canterbury, or other markets."

In other parts of southern and central England, Youatt describes:

Bedford: *"In the course of the summer, some Scotch and Welsh cattle are bought in... selling off in September and by the beginning of February the whole are disposed of."*

Berkshire: *"In the forest districts... many Welsh and Scotch cattle are grazed, and heavier cattle occupy the more fertile pastures."*

Essex: *"At some periods of the year these flats are covered with cattle, chiefly of the small kind, and mostly the Welsh or Scotch runts; indeed the grazing is principally confined to these small cattle."*

Isle of Wight: *"A few Welsh and West Country cattle bought each year."*

Leicester: *"...always occupied by a strange variety of beasts from Ireland, Scotland and Wales and every neighbouring county."*

Shropshire: *"...a few Montgomeries... and some other Welsh breeds are kept... generally in the hands of cottagers and small farmers, who purchase them because they are hardy, and will weather the winter... better than most other breeds. Great numbers of them pass through Shropshire on the way to the southern counties."*

Suffolk and Norfolk: *"(in addition to) ...Vast numbers of Galloways... A great many Welsh cattle, and a few Irish, are also grazed."*

As the towns of southern central England developed, the pattern changed, especially with the coming of the railways. The counties of Leicestershire and Northamptonshire became far more important for the Welsh drovers and were taking most of the cattle by the middle of the 19th century.

Young lads would play truant from school to earn money helping farmers take home cattle bought at Northampton Fair

Barnet Fair

Here on the northern fringes of London was held one of the country's largest cattle fairs. If St Faiths near Norwich was the main collection point for Scottish cattle, then without doubt Barnet was the Welsh Mecca. The enormous September fair here was called the Welsh Fair, at which large numbers of Welsh cattle and horses were sold.

Barnet fair was a great occasion with about 40,000 cattle being sold there in 1849. A tremendous noise and hubbub would have undoubtedly arisen from the nearby taverns and from the herds overflowing the surrounding common land. The grand ending of each fair was the Welsh drovers horse race, when men would race on the horses that they had ridden with the herds on the road from Wales. The prize was a saddle and bridle, bought by public donation, and great was the merriment and much the betting.

An interesting description of the types of horses and cattle sold here appeared in a report, originally in the *Daily News* and written by one who called himself a Midland County Farmer and was printed in the *Caernarfon and Denbigh Herald*, in September 1850:

"... the Welsh Horse Fair (Barnet), and a wilder or more noisy scene it is difficult to conceive. Always full, it was fuller than usual this year, and a brisk trade was driven by the Welsh horse drovers. These horses, which are of all sizes, are from one to four year olds, are not led, but driven, after the fashion of cattle. Few of them are more than imperfectly broken in, among them many useful horses are to be met with, and occasionally a very clever hackney. The way in which the Welsh jockeys throw themselves on the drove,

The great Welsh Fair at Barnet, 1849

A highlight of the Fair was the Welsh
drovers' horse race

single out a particular colt, drag him out and mount him for exhibition to a customer, is most amusing, the whole being accompanied by shouts and cracking of whips on the part of the master dealer and his group of helpers, who are commonly very numerous. Then when a sale has been affected, the whole band set up a tremendous shout.... Casting their hands and whips on high like so many wild men..."

"Beyond the Welsh horse fair and nearer to Barnet is the Welsh cattle fair. Here all kinds of Welsh cattle are to be met with; there are cows and heifers, yearlings and two year old heifer, and steers – 'runts' from two to four years old, at prices varying from £4 to £5 each and up to £9 and £11, and even higher. These cattle are generally black, and though small are kindly, well-shaped animals, which prove profitable where there's rough land attached to a farm on which they can run through the winter, and maintain, nay, improve their condition on a moderate quantity of food. They are much bought by farmers of Hertfordshire, Essex, Sussex, Kent and Middlesex, who let the larger beasts, the four-year olds, to run on their pastures and stubbles till November, where they generally get fresh, after which they are tied up and fattened off with corn, oilcake and turnips, or sometimes with hay and turnips, or hay and oilcake. The younger cattle are allowed to run through the winter in the rough pastures and are then either fed fat on grass during the summer, or finished off in the house the following year. Others buy Welsh heifers, keeping them at little cost during the winter, when they calve in spring, fat off their calves, and are kept in milk six or eight weeks longer, and are then dried and fed off. To a farmer having a large extent of rough pasture, and without much accommodation for house feeding, I do not know any sort of cattle likely to prove more profitable than well-selected Welsh beasts. They are good in quality when fat, and from their small size are very valuable."

A more lively account appeared in the *Farmer's Magazine* (1856):

"imagine some hundreds of bullocks like an immense forest of horns, propelled hurriedly towards you amid the hideous and uproarious shouting of a set of semi- barbarous drovers who value a restive bullock far beyond the life of a human being, driving their mad and noisy herds over every person they meet, if not fortunate enough to get out of their way, closely followed by a drove of unbroken wild Welsh ponies, fresh from their native hills all of them loose and unrestrained as the oxen that preceed them: kicking, rearing and biting each other amid the unintelligible anathemas of their inhuman attendants..."

Journey's end and getting paid

Having completed the journey and the animals sold, the hired men could now receive their payment. Those of a sensible nature would bring most of their money home for their families while the wilder elements would aim to sample the delights that the town or city had to offer just as enthusiastically as the American cowboys of the 1870s-80s upon reaching the railheads at Abilene or Dodge City. It is probably these men, frowned upon by the respectful chapel-going society back home that often gave a bad name to the droving profession. As the poet Twm o'r Nant described:

"...o dafarn i dafarn elai'r hen borthmon diofal,

...yn canu efo'r tanne, ac ymlid puteiniaid"

...from pub to pub went the care-free drover,

...singing to the strings and pursuing whores.

In most towns and especially in London there were plenty of distractions. Near the old Smithfield market were plenty of taverns, houses of ill-repute and the huge Bartholomew's Fair to tempt the unwary. A story in the *Daily News* (1850) describes a typical pitfall:

"A Welsh drover fell among the thimble-riggers at Barnet Fair, and was considerably fleeced. He, however had his revenge in the following fashion –

Quitting the town with his drove, he espied one of his plunderers in the road; with the assistance of a brother drover or two, he made capture of him, fastened him Mazzeppa-like [i.e. tied face down with his head above the horse's tail], *astride one of their wildest unbroken colts, started the animal off at a rough trot, and after a ride of four or five miles, the fellow galled, jaded, and three parts dead, was glad to purchase his release from further torment by disgorging his illgotten pelf."*

The head drover, now responsible for the sales money for his drove, would keep a sober head and a wary eye for those who would try to relieve him of his fortune. Being aware of the risks and a professional at his work, he would take the appropriate measures to ensure his own and the money's safe passage home.

Over Bwlch yr Oernant to Llangollen

Smithfield Market

The ultimate destination of most of the animals for the London meat market was Smithfield which, up to 1855 was located in the very centre of the city, near St Paul's Cathedral. An indication of the size and growth of the London market is given by the numbers of animals sold in Smithfield:[44]

Animals sold in Smithfield:

	1750	1790	1830
Cattle	70,000	104,000	160,000
Calves			22,500
Sheep	650,000	750,000	1,300,000
Pigs			255,000

By 1853 the number of cattle sold here had increased to 277, 000.

With such a large and growing market it is no surprise that it was well worth for drovers from Wales and other parts of the British Isles, including the Highlands of Scotland and Ireland to bring their beasts to supply the demand.

As the population continued to increase and industrialisation gathered pace through the 19th century, droving flourished. The English Midlands now became the main destination. Increased road traffic and housing developments around London meant that the Midlands were a more convenient destination, located between London and the increasingly populous towns of Birmingham and the 'black country'.

The relocation of Smithfield Market to Islington in 1855 served two purposes. One was to allow animals to be trucked directly to the market via the new Great Northern rail line. The other was to reduce problems arising from moving animals along the streets of the ever expanding city. Charles Dickens reported how criminal gangs would spook the cattle as a cover for young pickpockets to move in among the fleeing crowds. Specially licensed 'London drovers' were employed to ensure safe passage to Smithfield.

1. Smithfield Market 1845 in the centre of London. St Paul's Cathedral in the background; 2. Thomas Sidney Cooper 1827, cattle on the streets of London near Smithfield; 3. Cartoon illustrating fears concerning the re-location of Smithfield Market to Islington, 1855

Protecting the sales money

The drover, now charged with carrying the sales money back home, had to be prepared to defend himself against highway robbers and other types of thieves. Sometimes a pistol would be carried as drovers were exempt from the Disarmament Acts of 1716 and 1748 which made it illegal to carry such weapons. More frequently a blade in a stick or a strong cudgel would suffice as these could be brought into action immediately. Their full-time hired hands would frequently stay with them and they would, as a matter of course whenever possible, arrange to meet up with other drovers that they knew from their own home area and travel together.

The drovers of north Wales would be accompanied by their dog – a large strong cattle dog of the Welsh type who would defend his master against all comers. A bull-mastiff was frequently the animal of choice by drovers from the north of England, while in Germany a breed especially developed by drovers as a good working dog and for their own self-defence was the Rottweiler.

A story from Sarn Meillteyrn in Llŷn tells of a drover's dog called Tryg, who, when not working would be tied up in the barn. Tryg, however, unknown to the drover, had the habit of slipping his collar at night and going off on his own before returning at dawn and pushing his head back in. When a neighbour claimed that he'd seen Tryg attacking his sheep in the early hours they went to investigate and found not only that the collar was loose but muddy paws and blood around the mouth. Such proof of guilt meant that the dog had to be destroyed but before the men could return from the house with a shotgun Tryg had slipped his collar again and disappeared.

Shortly afterwards the drover was returning home from a droving trip without his trusty dog and followed a path through a woody vale. He needed to be wary of highway robbers and when a man suddenly appeared, blocking the path ahead, and several more from behind the trees he knew he was in trouble. Looking quickly around he saw that one of the men had a big dog with him – a dog he knew, it was Tryg! Trug must have followed his old familiar routes and been picked up by these men.

The drover quickly called: "Tryg! You've helped me before and you'll do it again! – *CYDIA nhw Tryg!!* (SEIZE them Tryg!)". Tryg duly obliged; scattering the thieves and saving his master and the money. He was now brought home a hero and for his good deed was forgiven his previous transgression. A new hole was put in the collar so he could no longer abscond to do mischief at night and he served his master well for many more years.[45]

1. The late Arfon Roberts, Ysbyty Ifan holding a drover's stick with blade inside;
2. Market stick with blade once owned by Owen Elias, Rhedynog, near Pwllheli

The Post and early drovers' banks

To avoid having to carry large sums, some drovers would post the money home on the Royal Mail stagecoach. This was a method used by the young sheep drover, Robert Jones of Llanystumdwy in the 1820s. Undoubtedly his father, who was also a drover, would have insisted on this and would meet the coach at Cricieth to receive the money. In Robert Jones' account books in the 1820s there are 22 references to money being posted home from the east of England, Wrexham and Chester. During the year and a half from July 1823 to February 1825 the sums posted amounted to almost £2,000.

A more secure way was to use the banking system which, in the latter part of the 18th century, after the monopoly of the Bank of England was broken, saw the proliferation of a large number of local banks, many of which were associated with specific trades. The banks provided security and many were located around or in the main market areas. Wilkins Bank in Brecon, established in 1778, was one well known for servicing drovers and dealers from a wide area. These included drovers from the English Midlands who converted their own local Midland banknotes to Brecon notes in order to buy cattle in Cardiganshire, Pembrokeshire and Glamorgan.[46]

In the late 19th century, banks from Llangefni would even open temporary branches complete with a cashier, cash-box and guard at local hostelries in Llanerchymedd on fair days in that village. The cashiers, guards and cash-boxes would return to Llangefni by train at the end of the day.

The drovers, with their need to safely transfer large sums of money over long distances, played an important part in the development of the early banking system and were responsible for setting up a number of banks. The most famous of these were:

Banc yr Eidion Du (**The Black Ox Bank**) – set up by the drover David Jones in the King's Head, Llanymddyfri in 1799. Officially known under the name 'David Jones & Co.', but best known from the illustration of a black ox on its banknotes.

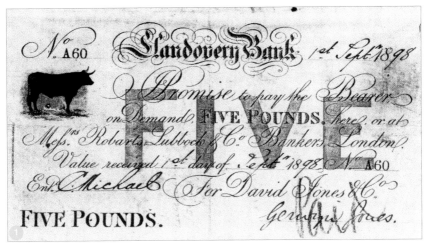

Branches were established at Lampeter and Llandeilo and the bank carried on until 1909 when it was taken over by another bank which had been set up by a Welsh family, the Lloyds family of Dolobran, under the sign of the Black Horse.

No bank enjoyed more local credit than the Black Ox Bank. It is said that during the run on banks in 1825, a client came to withdraw his money. The bank, in

1. *£5 promisory note of the Black Ox Bank*
2. *The King's Head, Llanymddyfri where the bank was founded*

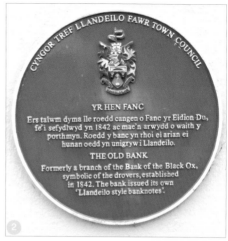

anticipation of a run against it, had just received a consignment of Bank of England notes, which the cashier handed to the depositor. He, however, refused these notes and demanded instead the notes of the Black Ox Bank.

Banc y Ddafad Ddu (**The Black Sheep Bank**) – officially the 'Aberystwyth and Tregaron Bank' but better known as the Black Sheep Bank because of the illustrations of a black sheep on its notes: one black sheep on its £1 note; two on its £2 note; one and two black rams respectively on its £5 and £10 notes and a black lamb on its ten shillings note. Opened in 1810, it only lasted five years before going bankrupt.

These banks, in addition to issuing their own distinctive signed and dated notes, would also authorise banking agents in London and elsewhere to issue promissory notes on their behalf. This allowed the drover to take his sales money to a bank which had an agreement with his home bank and exchange the cash for a promissory note. Such a note could only be cashed by the registered customer back

home which meant that if that note fell into the hands of a thief, it would be useless to him as he would be unable to cash it.

Promissory notes were a fairly secure way of moving large sums of money and would be incriminating evidence if found in the possession of a thief. A case in point follows a theft at the Three Rabbits Inn,

1. & 2. Later site of the Black Ox Bank, Llanymddyfri with blue plaque; 3. £2 promisory note of the Black Sheep Bank; 4. The Old Bank, Bridge Street, Aberystwyth with black sheep above the doorway

Mannor Park, London in 1785. This is the same Inn that John Roberts of Tŷ Cerrig stayed at in 1816 when he wrote home complaining about poor cattle prices and telling his wife to plant potatoes without expecting any help from him.[47]

The incident, described in the Essex Review (1941), was based on a contemporary account and, if anything, indicates not only the risks but also the large sums of money involved:

"A daring robbery was committed at the Inn in September 1785. According to a contemporary account, an agent for the Scottish and Lincolnshire cattle Salesmen from Gosfield came to the house one evening on his way to Smithfield Market, bringing with him £1,100 in bank notes and a purse containing 162½ guineas. He retired to bed soon after his arrival, leaving the money in a pocket of his breeches, which he placed beneath his head. A well-dressed youth slept in the same room, and during the night found means to abstract the notes and purse from underneath the owner's head and departed with his spoils before daybreak. At about seven o'clock the following morning the theft was discovered and information given at all the police offices in London. After a long search a beautiful young woman named Frances Davis was taken into custody and upon examination was discovered to be the same person who had stayed at the 'Three Rabbits' the previous day. A large part of the proceeds of the robbery were found concealed in her clothes. It was said she was connected with a large gang and had for some time been employed elsewhere in robberies of a similar nature."

The Three Rabbits Inn, Mannor Park, London

Highway Robbers

There were two types of highway robber that drovers and travellers had to contend with. One was what we would call today a 'mugger', being one or several fairly local men who would opportunistically prey upon people passing through their territory, and who usually killed their victim to prevent him identifying his attacker. The other was the 'classic' highway robber on horseback, with his more professional and gentlemanly demeanour, who wandered widely and usually did not kill his victims unless they resisted. The 'classic' highwaymen originated as Royalist officers who had lost their fortunes following the English Civil War (1642-1651) and had taken to the road specialising in stage-coach robberies, complete with pistols and a black mask. Some became folk-heroes and their 'gentlemanly' manners were emulated by other thieves up to the late 18th century.

Several stories have survived of drovers' encounters with highway robbers. Sometimes they won, sometimes they lost, but on the whole the instances are fairly uncommon because, as previously

'Muggers' frequently killed their victims to avoid being identified

mentioned, the drovers were professionals who knew the risks and could usually handle themselves well in dangerous situations.

Below is a selection of stories passed down orally over generations; most probably based on real incidents, but possibly with some embellishment:

Murder in Nant Ffrancon – In an account of the local histories of Llandegai and Llanllechid parishes published in 1866[48] we find a story about two thieves who attacked and killed two drovers from Shrewsbury, a father and son, on the shores of Llyn Ogwen above Nant Ffrangcon in 1670. They were on their way to buy cattle in Anglesey when they were attacked.

The fight was seen by a young shepherd boy further up the slope and who ran down to investigate. By the time he arrived the thieves had already killed the two drovers and were taking their money. The thieves now went after the boy to prevent him raising the hue and cry and pursued him up the slope. Because they were gaining on him the boy and his little dog hid in the great scree above the lake. The story describes how the thieves came looking for him and how one of them stood upon the rock the young lad was hiding under, clutching tightly the muzzle of his dog to prevent him from betraying their hiding place. Eventually the two murderers departed over the Glyderau towards Beddgelert and were never caught. This story was recorded nearly two hundred years later, being told by an old lady who was a descendant of the young boy who had hidden in the scree.

Attack on the Abergwesyn road – a wonderful account is preserved in a booklet: 'The Trail of the Black Ox' by George Horsey, published in the 1930s. He recorded the following story told by his

grandfather who used to run the famous Drovers Arms on Mynydd Epynt:

> *"The Tregaron to Abergwesin route and the Devil's Bridge route over the old Aberystwyth road, were subject to this danger, and ferocious attacks had been made on the drovers when it was known they were carrying large quantities of gold sovereigns to London.*
>
> *One tale was told, how the herd of cattle were going along the track between*

Trail of the black ox

Tregaron and Abergwesin, the guide in front of the herd reported that he suspected a highwayman high up on the hill, and it was .... arranged what action should be taken should he attack them.

When the herd came out onto the open hill, the drovers saw the highwayman cantering down towards them. When he got near he shouted to the Guide 'Hand over your Gold, or I shoot you!', the Guide called a foreign sailor who had run away from a foreign ship smuggling brandy into the Cardigan ports. The Guide gave the sailor a jean bag containing bits of metal ores, to give to the highwayman.

By this time three drovers had crept up to the front of the herd, taking cover behind the cattle. They carried catapults, with lead bullets in their pockets, which they shot at stray fowls, etc., on the roads when passing farms, which they cooked for supper at night.

When the sailor got near the highwayman, the drovers took aim and shot three bullets at the highwayman's black mask. Three bullets hit the highwayman in the head. He slumped in the saddle, and his pistol fell to the ground. The sailor ran and picked up the pistol

and shot at the highwayman, and the drovers pulled him off his horse, but he was already dead. The Guide searched the highwayman as the sailor shouted – 'Me no coat – plenty coats now', and the sailor stripped off and put the highwayman's clothes on.

The drovers took the saddled horse and the herd continued on their journey. The horse and saddle were sold when they got to Herefordshire, and the money was shared equally between the drovers."

Escape on the Migneint moor – a local story heard at Llidiardau tells how a drover returning home with a group of fellow drovers as far as Bala was obliged from there on to cross the Migneint moor alone to Llan Ffestiniog. He was wary of the crossing as the group had noticed that they were being followed at a distance by a lone rider on a fast horse. A fast horse being always the preference of a highwayman.

Having parted company with his friends at Bala the drover rode on quickly to the tavern at Llidiardau and arranged a ruse with the tavern-keeper to throw off his pursuer. The saddle was taken off the drover's horse in the stable and the animal

Pont y lladron on the edge of the Migneint moor

had been re-saddled and led, out of view of the tavern, a short distance up the road. He mounted and galloped off at high speed, thinking that he had shaken off his pursuer. However, a few miles on, he looked back only to see the other man riding quickly after him.

He now realised that he was in serious danger and took the only action he could think of. Coming to a bridge on the edge of the moor he dismounted and led his horse underneath. There they stood in the stream when the other rider galloped across and disappeared into the distance. The drover got back on his horse and rode back towards Llidiardau, to be met by a group of other riders who were coming to search for him. They decided to follow the highwayman across the moor to Llan Ffestiniog and found him in the Pengwern Arms. There, they captured him, dragged him out and beat the living daylights out of him, guilty or not, with a warning not to venture here again.

Some 'classic' highway robbers – while specialising in robbing stage-coaches, some of the well-known 'gentlemen of the road' were not averse to stopping anyone

fed and groomed. When the man following arrived shortly after, his horse was given the same treatment. The drover ordered a meal and likewise the other man. The drover's meal arrived fairly quickly and he made an excuse to leave the premises to visit a relative nearby and would be back shortly to fetch his horse. The other man's meal took more time to arrive and was much larger.

In the meantime the drover's horse

The Pengwern Arms, Llan Ffestiniog

who looked as if they could be carrying money, including drovers.

One of the most well-known and daring was Will Nevison (1640-1685). He operated on a considerable scale and ran a large gang of highwaymen covering the north of England from coast to coast. They partook in many robberies but also ran a protection racket – demanding 'insurance payments' from Scottish and north of England drovers for safe passage down south. They guaranteed that no other highwayman would attack them and would 'take out' any that ventured to do so.

Another was William Davies (1627-1690), a Welshman originally from the Wrexham area, the most long-lived and successful of all highwaymen. He took a farm on Bagshot Heath but diversified his occupation to include highway robbery which he pursued for 40 years before being finally caught and hung. He was a master of disguise which ensured his anonymity and it was a great embarrassment to his friends and family when Davies, otherwise known as the Golden Farmer because he was so rich, was eventually caught. Living among the farming fraternity he knew of their movements and when not robbing coaches on the Heath would, in disguise, even rob some of his own neighbours when he knew they were carrying money to buy cattle.

Dic Turpin (1706-1739) in his younger days was part of a gang in Essex which targeted farmhouses when they knew the farmer would be away buying cattle. They would torture and threaten the family into yielding up their valuables. When a fifty guineas reward was offered for the apprehension of the gang, they were either caught or fled. Turpin went north to start a short but dramatic career as a daring highwayman.

Wil Ddu of Rhandirmwyn – recorded on tape by Robin Gwyndaf of the Welsh Folk Museum in 1976, David Jones of Abergwesyn told the story of Ruth Watkins, a young girl from the district who, with two others, went to London in the company of drovers to work in the gardens. The party was held up by the notorious highwayman Wil Ddu (Black Will) of Rhandirmwyn. "Your money or your lives", he demanded, upon which the distressed girls said that they had none. "Well, I must have something off you, what about a kiss each?" he then said.

Ruth squared up and refused him, upon which he was so impressed with her spirit that he gave her a gold guinea and let them go on their way. Wil Ddu was eventually captured and hanged in Llanymddyfri for highway robbery some years later.

1. *Dic Turpin in full flight;*
2. *William Davis, alias The Golden Farmer robbing a traveller on a deserted heath*

The coming of the railways

In the 1850s-60s the railways began to play their part. From now on it would no longer be necessary to walk animals long distances as they could now be trucked to the Midland pastures quickly. This was kinder to man and beast and meant that animals in much better condition could be transported.

The first mainline railways came to Wales, servicing the north and south Wales coasts, in the late 1840s and early 1850s. But it was the 1860s which saw the greatest period of railway expansion when several different companies, e.g. the Great Western, Cambrian Coast, LMS and others opened a network which linked the Western parts of Wales with the English Midlands and large cities. This allowed a much easier passage for animals as they could now be trucked to their destinations in a single day rather than having to take 2-3 weeks on foot.

Animal transportation required special facilities in terms of carriages, marshalling yards for loading and unloading at each end and for feeding, watering and cleaning.

Once the system was in place the chance to reduce the overhead costs of tollgates, overnight accommodation etc. would not have been lost on drovers and cattle dealers. They quickly adapted their practices to benefit from the more cost-effective and quicker transport system which also opened up extensive new markets for their beasts.

An account of the first instance of trucking cattle from Bangor station[49] is to be found in the Welsh magazine *Cymru* by the cattle driver David Thomas from Caernarfon. He worked for the drover Rhys Williams of Denbigh and, with much trepidation, the two men loaded seven truckloads of cattle at Bangor for the long journey to Kent. Starting out at 7.00am the two men travelled with the cattle, not daring to let them out of their sight and checking their condition at every stop. They arrived in London at 4.00am the following morning and were met by William, Rhys's brother, an experienced man who guided the drove through the city before the traffic started. They were exhausted by mid-day, which was when they arrived in Eltham, Kent. To them, this was a miraculous journey considering that previously they had been obliged to take three weeks to do the same on foot. Soon, the over-carefulness of that first journey was replaced by a more casual approach, with the cattle and drovers traveling in separate carriages.

After 1850, when the tubular rail bridge connecting Anglesey to the mainland was opened, large numbers of Irish cattle began to be trucked to the English grazing counties, with their numbers increasing dramatically with the opening of new harbour facilities at Holyhead in 1880. Eventually this led many Anglesey farmers to regularly attend fairs in Ireland to purchase Irish store cattle for fattening on their own improved pastures.

After the branch-line to Llanerchymedd was opened in 1866, Anglesey drovers increasingly transported fattened cattle, sheep and pigs to Manchester. They would travel weekly in each other's company and formed a circle of friends known as '*porthmyn Manceinion*' (Manchester drovers) which operated at least up to the Second World War. Tom Richards of Llanfrothen in the old county of Meirionnydd became part of this fraternity and in the 1930s would walk stock from Llanfrothen to Maentwrog Road Station and truck them down the Conwy Valley line and on to Salford. He would return with his Anglesey compatriots, with a thick, tight wad of white £5 notes tied together with an elastic band in his pocket. Most of the cattle and sheep from Anglesey went directly to Manchester during this period and were a major source of the city's supply.

Further south, by the mid-1850s, the Great Western Railway had extended from Newport to Milford Haven via Carmarthen and Haverfordwest.[50]

Cattle being loaded onto rail trucks

The late 1850s and 1860s saw the extension of the main lines along the northern and southern edges of Wales by branch-lines heading southwards and northwards. This, coupled with and linking with westward extensions from various points along the north-south Chester to Newport line just over the border provided, by the late 1860s, direct links between much of the Welsh heartlands and the Midland grazing counties.

We can follow the change from treking on foot to trucking on rails in the account books of the Jonathan family of Dihewyd.[51] In the late 1830s-1840s they would walk their cattle droves all the way from west Wales to the Midlands and south-east of England. But after 1856 they abandoned the old Tregaron-Abergwesyn route to England through Herefordshire in favour of the turnpike from Aberystwyth to Mallwyd or Newtown and thence to Welshpool and the railhead at Shrewsbury. As the line progresses westwards the railhead for the Jonathans had moved closer to Newtown by 1861 and to Machynlleth by 1863.

The 'classic' period of droving cattle on foot for long distances was now quickly

1. Cattle pens at a railway station;
2. Cattle pens between the port and the railway at Holyhead

coming to an end, being revived for short periods as circumstances demanded, as in 1912 during the rail strike of that year. The droving of sheep long distances within

Wales however, e.g. from Tregaron to Rhuthun lasted up to the 1930s after which lorries began to take over as the main means of animal transport.

The internal movement of sheep on foot was to carry on where the rail routes were either non-existent or inconvenient. For example in the 1920s-1930s men would drive sheep from Montgomeryshire through Mallwyd and over Bwlch y Groes to Llanuwchllyn and on to Dyffryn Conwy.

An interesting story relates how one sheep became lame coming over Bwlch y Groes. The drover left the animal with a farmer in Cwm Cynllwyd, promising to fetch it on a later occasion. He was unable to do this until the following year when he again passed this way. When he retrieved his sheep, which in the meantime had produced a lamb, a deal was struck – the drover taking the sheep and the farmer keeping the lamb for his favour.

The Cambrian Coast Line crossing the Mawddach estuary at Y Bermo

Market changes

An important consequence of the coming of the railways was a change in marketing system and in the frequency and distribution of the traditional fairs from which drovers would obtain their beasts. The numerous village fairs spread over large areas of the countryside now began to decline in favour of more frequent and larger fairs in villages, towns and strategic locations along the railways. These were eventually super-ceded in the 20th century by weekly auction mart sales.

Advantage was taken of railway transport not only by drovers but also by English dealers who came to buy stock to truck out. They would engage the services of local men to translate on their behalf and seek out suitable stock on the farms. Local drovers often found it advantageous to provide accommodation and transportation for the dealer, translate when buying from farmers and help with managing and loading the beasts. In return, the dealer would take practically everything the drover could provide; the drover knowing exactly what the dealer required.

Sometimes things would not work out as intended. An interesting story is told of an English cattle dealer named Clark buying a milking cow in Sarn Meillteyrn in 1905 having been assured by the farmer through an interpreter that this particular animal was '*yn llaethog fel y môr*' (as bountiful as the sea). As it turned out, the cow was near the end of her milking cycle and dried up soon after being taken over the border. The next time Clark was in Sarn he reminded the farmer that his promise of the cow's bountifulness had not been realised. The farmer's reply was that he had not lied, but had not indicated whether the tide was on its way in or out.

Price haggling between drovers or dealers and farmers in fairs and markets carried on until the First World War. It was then, as a consequence of the U-boat blockade during the later part of the war that things began to change. Now, in the face of food shortages, agriculture was effectively nationalised, with the state running the system of food production and distribution and ensuring a fair share to all at affordable prices through strict food rationing. Cattle, milk, sheep, pigs, poultry and eggs were now taken to local centres, frequently based on existing railside marketing sites with trucking facilities. Here, professional auctioneers, now working under government control operated a Grading system with guaranteed good and stable prices for producers. Drovers and dealers facilitated a steady supply of animals to the system.

After the war, in 1921, when the free market was reinstated many of the auctioneering companies who had run the Grading for the government now set up auction marts, usually in the animal Grading locations which, previously, had been the sites of fairs and markets on the railway lines. The mart system involved competitive and public bidding between buyers and the animals would be weighed publically as they came into the sales ring to be sold. Weighing was very useful for dealers buying directly for the meat market.

The marts did not have a smooth ride initially. Some traditional fairs and especially horse fairs persisted for many years, but the main competition was from the drovers and dealers who bought stock directly from the farms. Comments in the newspapers in 1920, when many of the marts in Gwynedd were being established tell the story. A plea to support the new

1. *Welsh Black cattle at Market Harborough;*
2. *An early cattle lorry, J H Parry, Caernarfon, 1932*

Bryncir mart in the February 17th, 1920 issue of *Yr Herald Cymraeg* newspaper states:

> *"This is the way to get rid of people who travel around searching for advantage to buy animals at below their value from the unsuspecting".*

In September of that year the same paper reported:

> *"The market at Chwilog is somewhat unstable. There is such a good name for fat lambs from this district as to attract buyers from Manchester and Birmingham to come here to buy them privately".*

Dealers from England now became more frequent and many drovers, in addition to their normal practice of trucking stock directly to England, would act as local agents for outside dealers. Typically, Ralph Fox, from Sandbach near Crewe would come on a weekly basis either to Llanfrothen on the Tuesday or Trawsfynydd to stay with local drover associates. The local drovers knew exactly what Fox was looking for: old cattle, bulls and horses, and would have procured beasts for him from various sources. Tom Richards and Owen Williams, otherwise known as Now Foty, would take Fox to

Bryncir mart to buy more. At the end of the week he would move to buy at the mart in Dolgellau and from the Edwards family of Llwyn. He would send truckloads of animals home to Cheshire, returning home on the Friday and be there on the Monday to receive more which had been sent from Llwyn that morning.[52]

1. *Ralph Fox (centre, with straw hat) in Llan Ffestiniog, 1930s;*
2. *J H Parry & Sons cattle lorries, 1950s;*
3. *Large L E Jones of Rhuthun lorry with small Ifor Williams trucks, 2015*

Horse Fairs

Up until the 1940s, before the internal combustion engine usurped the all-important role of horses on the land and on streets, horse fairs retained their importance. Buyers would prefer to see a working horse paraded on the street or on the farm to see how well it moved and handled rather than displayed in the confines of a sale ring in a mart.

Dealers representing various commercial enterprises would regularly attend some of the big north Wales horse fairs: Cricieth, Ffair Borth (Menai Bridge), Abergele, Rhuthun and Wrexham in the 1920s-1930s:

Street horses – big 16-17 hand horses were required to pull delivery waggons for grocers and breweries etc. A matching pair with braided hair and bedecked with ribbons would be an impressive sight pulling a colourful brewery waggon. Obviously, the local drovers and dealers supplying their big English buyers would seek to procure separately two fine horses with a similar pattern and colour because they would get a better price for a matching pair.

Some of the dealers who came to the north Wales fairs included Tordoff from Shelby, Yorkshire looking for street horses for Bradford; Fred Cash from Manchester; Mr Furie, supplying Liverpool and Manchester, who had a saying: "Never buy in candlelight"

Many local men, like Jones-Williams of Corwen and Griffith Owen of Glanllynnau near Pwllheli were heavily involved in this trade and operated on a fairly large scale. Charlie Davies of Rhosydd (Rosset), Wrecsam frequently came to Glanllynnau,

Loading a pony and foal

knowing that Griffith Owen could be trusted to find the very best for him and would truck them out in special horseboxes holding 3-4 horses.

Tom Richards, Y Wern, Llanfrothen on one occasion in the 1930s bought eight shire horses in Cricieth fair, tied them together in a line, bridle to tail bridle to tail. He then lifted his young son onto the bare back of the lead horse, who then, in company with one of the farmhands, rode the line of horses the eight miles home.

Railway horses – Sir Robert Vaughan of Nannau near Dolgellau was one of the directors of the Great Western Railway and bought horses for the company. During a rail strike in the 1930s he decided to drive the train himself from Dolgellau to Bala. The gate at Drws y Nant however was closed against him by the strikers but he chose to drive through regardless, smashing the gate to bits.

Warbleton was another English dealer who came to fairs in north Wales and the borders. He regularly attended the Abergele horse fair in June, to buy horses which had been well fed over the winter and therefore strong to work on the railway.

Willie Wilde of Hoole, Chester came for large strong horses to work in the Liverpool docks in the 1930s. A saying of his was: "you want weight to shift weight". He had a reputation for honest dealing.

Further south the great horse fair at Llanybydder attracted buyers, like Tom Richards, Llanfrothen and others from north Wales.

Smaller horses – for riding and to work as pit ponies. Certain fairs, especially if near large extents of moorland were well known for ponies.

The drover Silvanus Evans of Llan Ffestiniog in the late 19th and early 20th century would take ponies grazing on the Migneint moors to the great fair at Wrexham to be sold as pit ponies in the Flintshire coalmines. Others, such as Fred Evans, Llanidloes (who was also a well-known sheep drover), Chadwick from Breconshire and Davies ('Davies Sowth') from Maesycwmer near Merthyr would come north looking for 14-15 hand ponies for the south Wales mines.

There is no doubt that Llangammarch Fair was the biggest pony fair in Wales in the 1930s, and famous throughout the British Isles. It rapidly declined however following the Army's decision to order all ponies off the Epynt hills when that vast moorland area was requisitioned for military training in 1940.

An interesting account by John Pyper in *Llangammarch Wells Past and Present* (2000), describes how, between the First and Second World Wars, many farmers in the area kept ponies, some of which took a great interest in them and kept hundreds:

"Very early on the day of the Fair, October 15th (unless it fell on a Sunday, when it would be on the Monday following), ponies and horses would be driven from all over the Epynt, Upper Chapel and Llanfihangel Nant Bran, and from further afield, Abergwesyn and beyond.

Pigs to be sold at Llanybydder. Note the nets over the carts to prevent the animals escaping

Dealers would come from all over the country, many arriving on the mail train which reached Llangammarch station at 6 am and then making for the Cammarch hotel for breakfast. They came from the south of England, Devon and Cornwall, Northamptonshire, Bedford, Stafford, Cheshire, Essex and Lincolnshire, some from Swansea and the South Wales valleys for ponies for the pits and some from Anglesey intending to sell them on to Irish dealers coming over to horse fairs there.

There were no auctioneers – buyers and sellers would haggle and when a deal was struck would clap hands on it.

Autumn Pony Fair at Llangamarch, Breckonshire

Payment would be in cash, at one time all gold sovereigns. Ponies of 11 to 12 hands would be bought for the Derbyshire pits or some could take up to 13 hands and South Wales pits might take farm horses up to 13 to 15 hands. They had to be four years old before they could go down the pits, so they were broken in at 2 – 3 years and sold as four-year-olds for about £5 to £10. (Heavier) working horses were about £35 or perhaps £40 for a good one.

Ponies and horses sold at the Fair were driven to Garth Station, where they had enough sidings to marshal the special trains needed with different boxes for ponies and heavy horses to take them to their different destinations. Village youngsters would help to drive them along the road to Garth, which was not easy as the foals were trying to break back to find their mothers. A dealer might look in his pockets and give a lad 6d for his help or 2/6d to ride on his quiet little pony in front of the foals to lead them to Garth.

Some dealers might stay overnight but they would be on their way the next morning to find more horses, perhaps at Llandovery or at Newbridge Fair, which followed on 17th October.

It seems that Llangamarch Fair survived through the last war and for three or four years after it but with the removal of the ponies from the Epynt range and the swift invasion of tractors to replace the working horses it was fading fast. By the last years of the 1940s it had disappeared, to be succeeded by the auction sales of ponies at Cwm Owen and Llanafan."

Further west the Llanybydder horse fair was one of the biggest with drovers and dealers from all over Wales and England.[53] Today it is one of the biggest in Europe for

Rywben horse fair at Tregaron, about 1905

ey Square, Llangefni.

ponies and cobs, attracting buyers from Britain, Ireland and the continent.

A farmer from near Chwilog made an interesting comment about the demise of the Cricieth horse fair in the early 1950s as farmers switched to tractors. His statement provides a good insight into the meaning of the term 'sustainability'.

"I remember the day after the fair, seeing truckloads of horses being taken on the line from Afonwen to Caernarfon on their

Llangefni Fair, early 20th century

way to England. The horses going out and the money coming in. A few years later there would be truckloads of tractors coming in to Pierce, Pwllheli (agricultural implement dealer) to be sold to farmers in Llŷn and Eifionydd. The tractors coming in and the money going out."

Breed improvements

The rail system not only produced a quiet revolution in the means of transportation and marketing of livestock but also had a dramatic impact on the quality and type of beasts preferred. Breed improvement now gathered pace. Up to the coming of the railways there had been little sense in producing well finished beasts and then walking them 200 miles.

It is probably no accident that in 1873, soon after the railways reached the western coasts of Wales, the first pedigree Herd-book for the Welsh Black Cattle breed was established.

'Sir Watkin', pedigree Welsh Black bull exhibited in county shows in NW Wales by W E Oakeley of Plas Tan y Bwlch, 1880s

The demand had always been for store animals for the rich old fattening pastures of the English Midlands or for partial stall-feeding on turnips over the winter in the south-eastern counties.

Richard Colyer in his 'Welsh Cattle Drovers' (2002) says:

"...the demand for hardy Welsh stock ... persisted throughout the (19th) century. That these 'unimproved' Welsh beasts were so highly prized, suggests that their performance, in terms of growth rate and ability to fatten on the superior nutritional regime of the Midland grazing pastures, may reflect the stimulus of compensatory growth arising from previous nutritional deprivation."

In other words, coming off the rough pasturelands of the Welsh uplands, the rate of 'improvement' seen in these animals when put out on good pastures was faster and greater than in any other type. This, combined with the leaner quality of the meat of upland animals generally, meant that the taste on the plate would be far superior.

One is reminded of the equivalent for sheep: Gervasse Markham, in his treatise "Cheape and good Husbandry" (1631), says of Welsh sheep: "...praised only in the dish, for they are the sweetest mutton", meaning that he obviously appreciated the meat but not the quality of the wool. There is also the well known description by Thomas Love Peacock (1785-1866):

"While the mountain sheep are sweeter
The lowland sheep are fatter."

By today such great strides had been made in stock rearing, breeding and pasture improvement generally that the quality of the beasts reared on the Welsh hills is unsurpassed anywhere. This is why Welsh lamb is probably the best in the world and that the meat of the Welsh Black cattle is as good as and even superior to the Aberdeen Angus. The difference in the relative popularity of these two types of beef being due to the Scots being cannier at marketing than the Welsh.

In 18th century England, following the pioneering work of Thomas Bakewell and others, a tremendous improvement had been seen in the quality of livestock breeds. Pedigree lines for cattle, sheep, horses and pigs, exhibiting the best breed qualities were established and these were subject to continuing selection for further improvements. There was also much experimentation with cross-breeding, to develop new types and to identify the crosses which combined the best qualities of both parents and conveyed hybrid-vigour to the progeny.

This worked well on good land which allowed the heightened genetic potential of the beasts to be maximised, but was woefully unsuccessful in the uplands and other unimproved areas where the land was not productive enough. Mountain farmers knew that one of the most important qualities in their animals was hardiness and that attempts to 'improve' them by crossing with a lowland beast invariably softened the progeny. They were conscious of the bitter experience of some, who had 'improved' their sheep in this way, only to lose them during the next hard winter to come along. Similarly with cattle, what would be the point of improving stock and then walking them 200 miles to a market where the demand was high for low cost store animals?

To some extent the drovers themselves, given the nature of the market, were to blame for the lack of improvement in the native types. They would invariably go for the best stock when buying off the farms, which would have been the animals necessary for the genetic improvement of the herd.

The railways, changed all that and set in train a series of developments in marketing, breeding and animal husbandry culminating in our modern livestock industry. Sheep, however, continued to be walked considerable distances within Wales right up to the mid-20th century when the advent of large livestock lorries finally put paid to the practice.

The mid-19th century was an incredibly dynamic period in British history involving industrial and economic development at home, imperial expansion abroad, fast population growth and increasing affluence. Rural estates were quick to respond to the increasing demand for food and the profits which could be made. Consequently, considerable sums were invested in agriculture. This led to substantial improvements to tenanted farms, frequently involving modifying existing buildings and erecting new ones according to planned layouts for farm yards. The estate Home Farms experimented with new farming methods to be implemented through annual tenancy agreements and introduced better quality bulls, stallions and boars to service their tenants' animals.

While the market for store animals from the uplands remained strong, estate farms and those on the better valley lands around Wales now began to produce fattened animals to be trucked out. Improved grass and home grown fodder production including turnips; the use of guano and lime; winter housing and the increasing use of supplementary feed brought in by rail were imperative to these developments, allowing the beasts to reach their potential cost-effectively.

It now made economic sense here in Wales, as in other parts of the British Isles, to improve the stock by better breeding. It is no accident that with the setting up of the rail network we see a much greater move towards the establishment of pedigree breed types other than those already improved in the better lands by the pioneer breeders of the 18th century. The Pedigree Herd Book for the Dairy Shorthorn breed had been the first to be established, in 1822, followed by the

Llanrwst 640415

BOB PARRY

MART LLANRWST *Dydd Sadwrn, Mai 8fed, 1993* *am 11.30* **ARWERTHIANT HOGIAU PENNANT** 450 o wartheg stôr x Charolais (rhai ¾ Limousîn) Y cyfan wedi'u magu gartref.	LLANRWST MART *Saturday, May 8th, 1993* *at 11.30 a.m.* **PENNANT BROS. SALE** 450 Charolais x Store Cattle (some ¾ Limousin) All Home produced.

Postcard advertising private sale in Llanrwst 1993

Hereford in 1846; the Devon in 1851; the Galloway and Aberdeen Angus in 1862; the Welsh Black in 1874 and 1883; the Scottish Highland in 1884 and the British Holstein (later Friesian) in 1909.

An indirect, if poignant reference to the importance of rail links is to be found in a sermon delivered in a Chapel in the Dysynni valley during the First World War. The minister compared how: "*One day there would be truckloads of cattle sent by the Tudors of Dolau Gwynion from the station at Tywyn for slaughter in England. Next day there would be truckloads of soldiers from the* (nearby) *military camp at Tonfannau for slaughter in France.*"

The 'Golden Age', depression and shift to milk production

The 1860s-1870s is frequently referred to as 'The Golden Age' of British agriculture, before the demand for cheap food led to massive importation, which undermined the agricultural industry at home. This trend, starting in the 1890s, was to precipitate a series of agricultural depressions which, with the exception of the First World War, was to last up to the late 1930s. During this period Britain was importing around two thirds of its food requirements.

A consequence of the competition from imported beef at this time led to a partial shift towards dairy production since milk especially had to be consumed fresh and was therefore not amenable to importation. Milk was also well suited to be transported by rail, which led to the counties of south-west Wales becoming the major supplier for the populated valleys of industrial south Wales and, increasingly, London and elsewhere. North and mid-Wales supplied Liverpool, Manchester and Birmingham.

Cardiganshire drovers had long recognised the importance of milk retailing in London and had begun to establish family members in town dairies even before the railway era. A dairy keeper in Greenford[54], when his herd was milked out, would walk them to Tewksbury. There he met his brother to exchange them for a second herd, which had been walked from their Welsh pastures.

The trend to establish town dairies in London accelerated after the development of railway links and even more by the turn of the century in the face of the agricultural depression. Cardiganshire families came to dominate the milk retail industry in London and Birmingham, a situation which was to last until the 1950s, when dairy keepers gradually changed to be corner shop owners and subsequently to hoteliers.

Welsh dairies in London during the first half of the 20th century

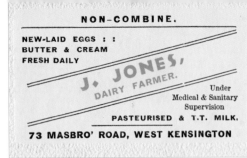

NON-COMBINE.

NEW-LAID EGGS : :
BUTTER & CREAM
FRESH DAILY

J. JONES,
DAIRY FARMER.

Under
Medical & Sanitary
Supervision

PASTEURISED & T.T. MILK.

73 MASBRO' ROAD, WEST KENSINGTON

Continued long distance walking of sheep

The last sheep drove on foot from Tregaron over the hills to England, to Harrow-on-the-Hill in Middlesex, occurring in 1900.[55] By this time almost all of the sheep sent to England were being trucked out by rail. Within Wales on the other hand the practice lasted for another half century. Here, significant markets were to be found between areas where rail transport was either inconvenient or not cost-effective. This meant that the walking of sheep over long distances, e.g. from Tregaron to Dyffryn Clwyd; Machynlleth to Brecon; Dolgellau to Llansilin; Llanbrynmair to Dyffryn Conwy etc., persisted up to the 1930s-40s, finally coming to an end in the 1950s when transportation in large stock-lorries took over.

An interesting account of such journeys is to be found in the magazine *Fferm a Thyddyn*,[56] where Gordon Edwards of Rhuthun, the fourth of five generations of drovers, describes his family's involvement. He relates how his grandfather, William Hugh Edwards, at the beginning of the 20th century, would ride from Penmaen, Dolgellau to Tregaron and as far as Nant Stalwyn at the headwaters of the Tywi to buy wethers. He would pay in gold sovereigns, having carried the money in hidden pockets in the saddle.

Having bought the animals, shepherds from Tregaron would drive the animals as far as Eisteddfa Gurrig – wethers are notoriously difficult to drive from their cynefin. Men from Penmaen would meet them at Eisteddfa Gurrig to take them on to Llanbrynmair, the animals being tired and easier to handle by now. Onwards through Mallwyd and past Dinas Mawddwy to Dolgellau. There, at Llwyn, they would be rested before resuming their journey to farms around Llangernyw and Llansannan in Denbighshire to eat swedes over the winter in order to fatten by the spring. A butcher from Llandudno was their final customer.

1. Sheep at Aberglaslyn, 1920s; 2. Sheep crossing the bridge at Llandeilo, early 20th century; 3. Bill Phipps droving sheep from Buckinghamshire to Guilsborough, 1919

In spring the Edwards family would buy yearling sheep which would be walked to fairs in Brecon. Similar journeys were made by the drover Dafydd Isaac of Trefenter who regularly undertook the 90 mile trek from Machynlleth to Brecon, with 300-400 sheep, in the early decades of the 20th century.[57] Other drovers from the Llanddewibrefi region regularly drove both cattle and sheep to Brecon Fair in the years before the 1939-1945 War.[58]

An important element in the business of the Edwards family during this period was buying sheep from farms over a wide area of Meirionydd and Montgomeryshire and bringing them to Llwyn before sending them on to Dyffryn Clwyd. There they would be sold in private fairs at Gwyddelwern, Cynwyd, Dinbych (Denbigh), Henllan or Caerwys. Walking around 3,000 sheep to these fairs was easier in those days since there was very little traffic on the roads in comparison to today.

Having reached Y Bala at the end of the first day the sheep would be turned into fields owned by the Red Lion and the men would stay in the tavern. Next morning they would travel to Sarnau, turn the sheep into a large field at the top of the pass, still known as *cae tair mil* (3,000 field) and have lunch at the The Boot tavern (now closed). Onwards to Gwyddelwern and elsewhere where private sales were made to local farmers.

Some examples from the Edwards family accounts records the sale of 3,832 ewes at Gwyddelwern on October 5th, 1917. These sheep would be kept until the following year, by which time they had strengthened after their mountain upbringing and be ready to take the lusher pastures of Dyffryn Clwyd. They would now be bought back and moved further up the valley, as three days after the fair at Gwyddelwern, on October 8th, 1917 they would be selling in a fair at Henllan. Twelve days later the men had been back to Dolgellau, returning to Cynwyd with another drove of almost 3,000 to be sold there on October 20th.

Such journeys on foot lasted up to the 1930s while the movement of sheep to Dyffryn Clwyd and elsewhere still persists today by lorry.

Flocks of sheep being driven past Llyn Dinas, Beddgelert

Modern developments in agriculture

The 20th century witnessed a greater rate and degree of change in agriculture than any other period throughout history. Watershed periods were the 1940s-1950s when horses were replaced by tractors accompanied by their whole family of new implements, and the 1950s when the Rural Electrification Scheme brought electric power to farms throughout Wales. These innovations transformed the agricultural industry making it very different from the labour intensive mixed farming of yesterday and impacting directly on the production of animals.

A significant driving force for change was the increasing role of government in shaping agricultural developments. Thus, following the 1939-1945 War, the 1947 Agriculture Act brought in subsidies to guarantee and stabilise prices; grants for buildings improvement, liming, drainage etc., while the Agricultural Development and Advisory Service (ADAS) provided free advice, conducted research on experimental farms, held public lectures, farm demonstrations and a free testing service for soil fertility and animal feed quality.

ADAS advisers were to play an important part in facilitating change, coupled with the development of agricultural colleges to train young farmers in new techniques and systems. Farmers were quick to grasp the new opportunities and adapted their production methods accordingly. More productive varieties of grasses and clovers from the Welsh Plant Breeding Station, Aberystwyth came into general use, along with better breeding, feeding and houseing. Thus were laid the foundations of our modern more intensive pastoral systems.

The period, 1955-84, is sometimes referred to as the Production Era which was no less than a modern agricultural revolution. Some major developments in this period included:

- New machinery and technologies developed for practically every job/craft
- New high yielding grass and cereal

1. Welsh Black cow, Rhinogydd; 2. Welsh Mountain ram

varieties dependent on high fertiliser inputs

- Silage, in pits initially and big bale silage from the 1980s and feed blocks for sheep
- Bigger farm buildings/sheds for wintering cattle and indoor lambing
- Better animal husbandry and advances in veterinary care
- Crossing with selected bulls by artificial insemination especially in dairy herds brought rapid advances in animal breeding and crossing for increased production.

In the uplands the value of the Welsh Black cattle breed has long been recognised not only for being good beef producers but also for milking – a dual purpose breed in other words featuring highly in the dairy production of small to medium sized mixed farms in upland Wales in the 1950s. This made them ideal for crossing with lowland bulls because the Welsh Black's good milking capacity provides young cross-bred calves with the start they require, allowing them to thrive on less favourable upland pastures. The Welsh Black x Hereford cross, characterised by its black body and white face became very popular, combining the better quality of the beef with faster growth and more of it.

Similarly, crosses with Suffolk and Border Leicester rams in the uplands, or Wiltshire rams on Anglesey, became commonplace. A significant demand for half-bred ewes grew in the hilly areas of the border and south-western counties of England. From these, quarter-breds would be produced, retaining at each stage a diminishing degree of the high quality and hardiness of the Welsh mountain animals. Welsh drovers and dealers were heavily involved in this trade.

Following entry into the EEC in 1973 new crosses with continental breeds became popular, notably Charolais and Limousin – the calves again benefitting from the good milking capacity of their upland mothers. The demand for Welsh Black mothers for this purpose quickly developed in other upland areas such as Cumbria and western Scotland generating new marketing opportunities. Thus by the late 20th century, the major sales for Welsh Black breeding stock were to be found in Dolgellau and Carlisle, attracting buyers from the length of the western uplands of the British Isles.

In the 1980s the British government and EEC encouraged smaller farms in 'marginal' and upland areas to amalgamate in order to create larger and more efficient and intensive units. Upland farmers now began to buy nearby lowland farms and have come to own up to three or four in many cases by today. This allows them to complete the production cycle of rearing stock on their improved upland pastures and finishing them on their lowland properties.

Auction mart at Bryncir 1984

Modern day droving

The agricultural revolution of the second half of the 20th century has certainly impacted on the modern drover/dealer's business; not so much on the fundamental nature of his work, which is the movement of animals along a chain of supply, but in the various elements which make up that function. The quality of livestock dealt with has certainly improved, both for store and finished animals while the introduction of an ever increasing variety of continental breeds has greatly coloured hillsides and marts across Wales.

The animal trade today covers a much greater geographical range than ever before, with some large scale drovers and dealers buying and selling through the length and breadth of the British Isles. They will be familiar with every sale and mart throughout Wales and most of Scotland and England with a volume of trade involving turnovers of several hundred cattle per week and many thousand sheep and lambs in response to seasonal demands.

The digital age has also made its mark. Mobile phones are continuously in use, and a seller may even choose to post video images of the beasts on offer to potential customers. Once a deal is concluded transportation and payment may also be arranged online. Nothing, however, can replace direct personal contact on the farm or in the mart since it is here that social and market intelligence is gained by all sides, cementing business relationships and trust as has always been the case. Similarly, personal contact with regular customers on their grazing lands in England allows the experienced drover to know and be able to supply exactly what the customer wants. The drover's role is thus assured and will probably remain so as long as the demand for meat exists.

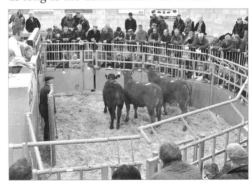

Modern day marts at Welshpool

Footnotes

[1] *Cannwyll y Cymry*, 1681

[2] *Trioedd Taliesin*

[3] PG Hughes, *Wales and the Drovers* (1988), p. 46

[4] KJ Bonser, *The Drovers* (1970, p. 42

[5] K Williams Jones, *The Meirioneth Lay Subsidy Roll 1292-3* (1976)

[6] AD Carr, *Medieval Anglesey* (1982)

[7] *The Welsh Cattle Drovers*, Richard Colyer, 1st Ed. (1976), p. 42

[8] Caroline Skeel, *The Cattle Trade Between England and Wales in the 15th to 18th Centuries*, Trans. Roy. Hist. Soc. (1926)

[9] R Colyer (1976), p. 42

[10] *Gwaith Guto'r Glyn* (1939), Ed.: J.Ll Williams & Ifor Williams

[11] R Colyer (1976)

[12] Council of the Marches, 1617, in: *Welsh Cattle Drovers*, Richard Colyer (2002), p. 64

[13] *Calendr of Wynn Papers* (1926)

[14] R Colyer (1976), p. 42

[15] J. *Meirionydd Hist. Soc.*, 3 (1960), p. 364

[16] *Calendar of Wynn Papers* (1926)

[17] R Colyer (1976), p. 44

[18] Lewis Lloyd, Coleg Harlech, pers. com.

[19] Twm Elias, *Y Porthmyn Cymreig* (1987)

[20] *Llafar Bro*, 108 (1985

[21] Megan Hayes, *Llwybr Llaethog Llundain* (2014)

[22] Twm Elias, *Y Porthmyn Cymreig* (1987)

[23] *Atlas Sir Gaernarfon* (1977)

[24] Lewis Lloyd, lectures at Plas Tan y Bwlch (1983-1986)

[25] Twm Elias, *Y Porthmyn Cymreig* (1987), p. 15

[26] *Hanes Bro Trawsfynydd* (2012)

[27] Twm Elias, *Gwartheg/Cattle* (2000)

[28] W Youatt, *Sheep* (1837)

[29] *Y Ffynnon* 66 (1982)

[30] R Colyer, *Welsh Cattle Drovers* (2002), p. 87

[31] www.localdroveroads.co.uk/background-history

[32] John Williams Accounts, late 18th century, taking 113 cattle from Bala to Billericay in Essex

[33] Jonathan Accounts, 1862

[34] Twm Elias, *Llafar Gwlad* 79 (2003)

[35] R Avent, Southampton, pers com

[36] *Y Cymro** (undated)

[37] R Avent, Southampton, pers com

[38] R Colyer (1976), p. 49

[39] RT Jenkins, *Y Ffordd yng Nghymru* (1933), Colyer (2002) for routes through mid and south Wales

[40] R Colyer, *Welsh Cattle Drovers* (2002)

[41] *Essex Fairs and Markets*, (1981)

[42] *Trans. Meirion. Hist. Soc.* (1956), p.311

[43] Lewis Lloyd, *Bwletin 3*, Gwynedd Archive Services (1976)

[44] based on: W Youatt, *Cattle*, 1832

[45] Twm Elias, *Llafar Gwlad*, 80 (2003)

[46] RO Roberts, *Brycheiniog*, VII (1961), p. 65

[47] (see page 76)

[48] Huw Derfel, *Hynafiaethau Llandegai a Llanllechid* (1866)

[49] Emlyn Richards, *Porthmyn Môn* (1998) p. 301

[50] R Colyer, *Welsh Cattle Drovers* (2002), p. 109

[51] R Colyer, *Welsh Cattle Drovers* (2002)

[52] Gordon Edwards, *Fferm a Thyddyn* 20 (1997), p. 35, and 39 (2007), p. 4

[53] Evan Jones, *Cerdded Hen Ffeiriau* (1972)

[54] www.localdroveroads

[55] Evan Jones, *Cerdded Hen Ffeiriau*, 1972, p. 29

[56] *Fferm a Thyddyn*, 20 (1997), p. 33

[57] Richard Philips, *Ar Gefn ei Geffyl* (1969)

[58] R Colyer, *Welsh Cattle Drovers* (2002), p. 124